"Put down whatever you are readi
Put. It. Down. And pick up this in
'Best Places to Go' in education innovation. Ted Dintersmith's journey shows us where corporate reformers got
lost and points to our constant educational true north:
trust, relevance, discovery, joy, and, above all, a purpose
that has nothing to do with a test score and everything to
do with developing the infinite potential of the creative,
critical mind and the compassionate, ethical character.
Every person needs to read this wonderful and important
book."

—Lily Eskelsen Garcia, President of the
National Education Association

"Ted Dintersmith took a serious education road trip and
came away with a message of hope, which this book presents through the stories of scores of fearless educators
around the United States who dare to do things better every
day. This is a must-read for anyone who wants to know what
school could be."

—Pasi Sahlberg, author of *Finnish Lessons 2.0*
and *FinnishED Leadership*

"Ted Dintersmith fuels a vitally important discussion
about the need to transform education and provide more
team-based, experiential learning opportunities to prepare students for the twenty-first-century economy. Dintersmith fosters a dialogue for sharing best practices and
harnessing new approaches that will yield tangible results
for students."

—Doug Burgum, Governor of North Dakota

"All children love to learn: they don't all get on with school. The problem isn't the children: it's how we do school. As Ted Dintersmith shows in this landmark book, it's not only possible to reimagine education, it's vital that we do. Too often schools are snagged in a corrosive web of tangled regulations, political agendas, outmoded institutional habits and a repressive culture of standardized testing. But there's hope. In among the undergrowth, there's an emergent counter culture of inspirational schools that are rising to the real challenges of educating young people for life in the 21st century. *What School Could Be* is a both vivid account of this grassroots revolution and a hard-headed analysis of its desperate significance. Above all it is a passionate manifesto for forms of education that do justice to the deep talents and diverse futures of all our children. It's essential reading for anyone who cares about young people and their education: and that should be everyone."
—Sir Ken Robinson, Author/Speaker, with new book *You, Your Child, and School*

"From the country's best schools to its worst, Ted Dintersmith has been there and reports what he's seen with a critical eye and a compassionate heart. His findings will surprise you, infuriate you, and, most of all, inspire you. Filled with amazing stories and extraordinary conversations, *What School Could Be* is hands down the best book on education that I've read in a very long time. Read it and act!"
—Tony Wagner, Expert in Residence at the Harvard Innovation Lab and author of *The Global Achievement Gap* and *Creating Innovators*

"*What School Could Be* shares thought-provoking stories about critical, positive changes happening in schools across the country. As Ted Dintersmith shows, and as I have seen in New Hampshire, empowering teachers in existing public schools allows them to arm students with the tools they need to succeed. These examples can help all policymakers focus on what actually works as we move this important discussion forward."

—U.S. Senator Maggie Hassan

"*What School Could Be* is a thought-provoking and inspiring look at our education system, from the perspective of an innovation expert who spent thousands of hours listening to and learning from great teachers all across our country. This book combines an incisive critique with insightful examples of exhilarating education. It will inform you, challenge you, and — hopefully – move you to action. A must read for anyone who cares about our children and the future of our nation."

—Linda Darling-Hammond
CEO, The Learning Policy Institute

"Ted Dintersmith's year-long journey gives us tremendous insight and hope about what works to create and sustain powerful schools. In highlighting educators who are 'doing better things' to uplift children's life prospects, he reveals very practical ways of strengthening public education."

—Randi Weingarten, President of the
American Federation of Teachers

"Very few books can leave you feeling both mad as hell and hopeful. This is one of them. Dintersmith has focused all his considerable passion, energy, and intellect on understanding the many ways that our educational system is broken, and how it can be fixed. We're failing our kids and our country, and we can do a lot better. Read this book to learn how."
—Andrew McAfee, cofounder of the MIT Initiative on the Digital Economy and coauthor of *Machine | Platform | Crowd* and *The Second Machine Age*

"*What School Could Be* is an inspiring and deeply moving tour of the best in American education. Even better, our guide is the tireless and thoughtful Ted Dintersmith. As the journey progresses, it becomes a compelling meditation on learning, human potential, and the power of the human spirit. If you care about our future, read and share this book."
—John Merrow, former PBS NewsHour education correspondent and author of *Addicted to Reform: A 12-Step Program to Rescue Public Education*

"If you want to understand what education looks like now and what it can and should look like in the future, start with this book. It's lively, accessible, smart, clear-eyed, and free from the partisanship that clouds so much of the discussion in education."
—James E. Ryan, Dean of the Harvard Graduate School of Education

"This is a must-read for anyone looking to understand

how our education system is impacting students in all fifty states, and the path forward to a better future."
—Adam Braun, New York Times bestselling author and CEO of MissionU

"*What School Could Be* is a powerful book that will inspire parents and teachers by showing how genuine, determined, and sensitive change can actually be achieved."
—Nancy Faust Sizer, coauthor of *The Students Are Watching*

"*What School Could Be* presents relevant, practical ideas backed by a huge number of examples of the innovative practices and programs taking place in schools across the United States. Ted Dintersmith also provides an essential critique of standardized tests and makes a huge contribution by showing why the idea of 'college for all' is false."
—Anthony Cody, author of *The Educator and the Oligarch: A Teacher Challenges the Gates Foundation*

"This is a critically important book that every educator should read and use. It offers a bold and credible account of why change is desperately needed in our schools—and how it's actually happening."
—Brad Gustafson, elementary school principal and author of *Renegade Leadership: Creating Innovative Schools for Digital-Age Students*

"*What School Could Be* is a powerful reminder that the future of 21st learning is already there. We just need to become better at getting the good ideas out of the classroom into the education system - rather than keeping education systems busy pushing old ideas into classrooms. What makes the book special is that it conveys its message through so many innovative and yet concrete and replicable examples that will challenge anyone in whatever context to step back and reimagine education."

—Andreas Schleicher, Director for the Directorate of Education and Skills at OECD

"Everyone tells us the education system is broken, and everyone has a pet theory about how to fix it. Ted Dintersmith did something different: He listened. He spent a year visiting 200 schools in all 50 states -- observing, asking questions, and in the process, changing his mind about many things. And what he brought back from his journey is precious: Hope. And direction. In dozens of schools across the country -- schools neither private nor rich -- smart leaders have already solved our nagging problems. What we need, nationally, is simply to be more like ourselves at our own best moments."

—Dan Heath, co-author of *Made to Stick, Switch,* and *The Power of Moments*

"*What School Could Be* is uplifting. It bolsters the case of teachers everywhere, validating their diligent, dedicated, and determined efforts to help their students grow, learn, and achieve."

—Jeffrey Huguenin, elementary school principal

"Dintersmith has put together the why, the what, and the how in one place. The stories of innovation he profiles are powerful reminders that these are not fanciful utopian ideas, but already exist in remarkable classrooms across our country. It's an important book for us all to read."
—Deborah Meier, author of *In Schools We Trust* and *The Power of Their Ideas*

What School
Could Be

What School Could Be

Insights and Inspiration from
Teachers across America

Ted Dintersmith

STEAL THESE IDEAS

Hardcover Edition Published by Princeton University Press

All Rights Reserved

Library of Congress Control Number: 2017956534
ISBN: 978-0-691-18061-8
ISBN: 978-0-578-50443-8 (pbk)

British Library Cataloging-in-Publication Data is available

Editorial: Vickie Kearn and Lauren Bucca
Production Editorial: Ellen Foos
Text design: Carmina Alvarez-Gaffin
Jacket design: Kathleen Lynch/Black Kat Design
Jacket photos: ©iStockphoto
Production: Erin Suydam
Copyeditor: Jenn Backer

This book has been composed in Archer & Minion Pro.

Printed on acid-free paper. ∞

Printed in the United States of America

10 9 8 7 6 5 4 3 2 1

If we teach today's students as we taught yesterday's, we rob them of tomorrow.
—John Dewey

The philosophy of the schoolroom in one generation is the philosophy of government in the next.
—Abraham Lincoln

Contents

Prologue

A few years ago, I connected some dots. Machine intelligence is racing ahead, wiping out millions of routine jobs as it reshapes the competencies needed to thrive. Our education system is stuck in time, training students for a world that no longer exists. Absent profound change in our schools, adults will keep piling up on life's sidelines, jeopardizing the survival of civil society. While not preordained, this is where America is headed. Yet few understand.

A looming crisis makes you do the unusual. I've done my share. For starters, I organized the documentary *Most Likely to Succeed* (*MLTS*), an official selection of two dozen leading film festivals including Sundance, and screened in over four thousand communities around the world. I teamed with education thought-leader Tony Wagner to write the book *Most Likely to Succeed: Preparing Our Kids for the Innovation Era*. Both the film and the book address the urgent need to reimagine education for the innovation era.

As these works gained traction, I started getting invited to speak to groups. Various aspects of my background helped me connect with audiences. My career spans business and public policy (start-ups, venture capital, congressional staff, U.S. delegate to the United Nations). I'm a parent of two recent high school graduates. I grew up in very modest circumstances and was the first in my family to go to college. I respect the practical (my dad was a carpenter), as well as the liberal arts (I majored in physics and English). And I love meeting teachers, who in turn seemed to appreciate a businessperson who advocates for trusting them.

Like so much in life, one thing led to another. Amid so many stimulating discussions, I kept getting questions I couldn't answer. How can one person make a difference? How can an existing school transform itself? Where do we begin? These questions, from people who care deeply, gnawed at me.

So I took a trip.

Not just any old trip. I did something unusual in education, maybe without precedent. I was on the road for an entire school year. I went to all fifty states, convened a hundred community forums, visited two hundred schools of all types, and had a thousand meetings. I spent 245 nights in hotel rooms and endured 68 TSA pat-downs. I met people of all ethnicities in communities reflecting America's full range of financial circumstances—the very poor, the poor, the becoming poor, and the affluent. I met those with real education power; I drew daily inspiration from teachers and students.

This trip was like drinking from a fire hose. In retrospect, my innovation career helped me process the deluge. Having worked with young adults as they navigate the innovation economy, I can recognize learning experiences that help build essential skill sets and mind-sets. Having lived through waves of disruption, I have a good sense for change models that work and ones that fail. This frame helped me make sense of a long, sprawling trip.

When I left home in the fall of 2015, I wasn't sure what I'd learn. But learn I did. All across the country, I met teachers and children in ordinary circumstances doing extraordinary things. I saw a mosaic of innovative classrooms and the conditions that let them blossom. In every community, I found sparks of learning that are so, so promising but reach only a sliver of our kids. They're everywhere and nowhere. While a single spark is an anecdote, an aggregation suggests something more—a vision for the future of school, inspired by innovative teachers across America. It's a vision that's powerful, that's achievable, and that just might enable our country to claw its way back from the brink and preserve the American Dream. It's a vision of what school could be.

FIGURE 0.1. Destinations on My Long Education Trip.

In the pages ahead, you'll cross America to see powerful examples of learning—in classrooms, in after-school programs, and in places you don't think of as school. From Atlanta to Anchorage, from Baltimore to Boise, from Concord to Cedar Rapids, and right on down the alphabet. For the most part, I let the educators tell you their stories. Keep in mind, though, that I met *all* of these inspiring people *in just one school year*, which speaks volumes about the expansive creativity of our teaching force. At first blush, these approaches seem disparate, even incoherent. But as the months rolled by, common principles emerged. Students thrive in environments where they develop:

- **Purpose**—Students attack challenges they know to be important, that make their world better.
- **Essentials**—Students acquire the skill sets and mind-sets needed in an increasingly innovative world.
- **Agency**—Students own their learning, becoming self-directed, intrinsically motivated adults.
- **Knowledge**—What students learn is deep and retained, enabling them to create, to make, to teach others.

We'll call these the PEAK principles—purpose, essentials, agency, knowledge. They abound in preschools, kindergartens, and Montessori schools—places where children love school, learn deeply and joyously, and master essential skills. We find PEAK cultures in our innovative businesses and nonprofits, where employees have the agency to discover and invent. But we don't find PEAK in most schools, from elementary grades through the cavernous lecture halls of college. In the typical American classroom, students are told what to study and when to study it. They cover content, rather than develop anything essential. They're pushed to jump through hoops and outperform peers, hollowing out any sense of purpose. Even top academic achievers retain little from their coursework. Anti-PEAK.

Conditions matter. We'll see the upside when schools are trusted to adopt PEAK. We'll understand how America talked herself into policies that shoved PEAK out of our classrooms, jeopardizing millions in an attempt to leave no child behind. We'll face findings you may find implausible, even preposterous, including:

- Today, the purpose of U.S. education is to rank human potential, not develop it.

- "College ready" impedes learning and innovation in our K–12 schools.
- All students would benefit from considerably more hands-on learning.
- We're trying to close the wrong achievement gap.
- We can make education better and more equitable by challenging students with real-world problems.
- K–12 schools, done right, would produce graduates better prepared for life than most current college grads.
- Educators can transform schools at scale with change models that establish conditions, rather than mandate daily practice.

I understand if you're skeptical, since this flies in the face of conventional education wisdom. Keep an open mind, though, as we visit the front lines of the battle for the heart and soul of our schools. Be inspired by children mastering what enables them to flourish. Observe learning conditions that prepare students to capitalize on, rather than be victimized by, machine intelligence. Be blown away by innovative teachers bucking a system to show us the way forward. We're going to learn from them.

My trip coincided with the 2016 presidential campaign, a bipartisan meltdown of anger and vile. Thankfully, there's nothing partisan about education. In the pages ahead, we'll meet dyed-in-the-wool conservatives and bleeding-heart liberals who agree, vehemently, on education priorities. But today's America is long on vehemence and short on agreement. The presidential campaign revealed a population unable to solve problems collaboratively. A society breaking down as it struggles to analyze critically, to debate thoughtfully, to seek and value truth. A civil society that's beginning to fracture.

America's future is in jeopardy. Our education model is wholly out of touch with today's world. Our country, unwittingly, is feeling the rumblings of two very different revolutions—the one we need, and the one we fear. If we have the courage to revolutionize education, our children will find their strengths, create fulfilling paths forward, and attack the many problems we're dumping on their laps. Or we can continue to make excuses for not reimagining school. Keep feeding children into an education machine that churns out young adults lacking meaningful skills and purpose, primed to throw hand grenades into the ballot box, or worse.

Is This Book for You?

Like most authors, I think everyone should read my book. If in fact the future of civil society hangs in the balance, perhaps they should.

This book will make open-minded adults step back and rethink education. If you're involved with a school, this book will spark ideas for advancing student learning. If you live abroad, you'll appreciate what foreign education leaders tell me: "We get our best ideas from America. The difference is that we act on them, and you don't." This book offers a tapestry of great ideas. Have at them.

If you're leading the charge to transform your school, this book can help you recruit allies. Share it with colleagues, friends, even strangers. Form a book club. Read it in conjunction with watching the film *Most Likely to Succeed*. You'll be surprised at how many in your community will respond to an aspirational vision.

If you're a parent, this book furthers your understanding of school's impact on your child. You'll start seeing things differently, and you'll be a better advocate. When it comes to shaping your child's values and life prospects, you need the broadest context, and so does your child.

I'm deeply grateful to our teachers. This book is yours. It springs from your creativity. Teachers are often depicted as indifferent, even lazy—like those caricatures in the misguided documentary *Waiting for Superman*. Well, I've been all over the country and have met thousands of teachers chomping at the bit to innovate. This book supports you. For teachers open to innovating, this book will encourage you to put a toe in the water, maybe even an entire limb. And if you teach traditionally, this book may persuade you to tolerate, even cheer on, your innovative colleagues and their chaotic classrooms.

I desperately hope this book reaches those who occupy education's commanding heights—legislatures, departments of education, testing and curriculum organizations, and college admissions offices. You need to hear this. Our children should study what's important to learn, not what's easy for you to test. School should develop each child's unique potential, not rank it for you with high-stakes standardized tests of low-level skills. Please, please, please consider the possibility that our innovative teachers, not data-driven policies, can best lead the way.

As we get ready to cross America, here's what lies ahead.

1. **Conventional Schools and Their Contexts:** We visit the type of school most adults went to. Based on a century-old factory model, this particular school excels in preparing children for a world that no longer exists. It's torn between two contexts: an education system anchored in the past and an innovative world defining the future.

2. **Real Gold amid Fool's Gold:** We'll see stunning examples of classrooms where children love school as they develop purpose, essential competencies, agency, and deep knowledge. PEAK.

3. **Prepared for What:** In a country as large and diverse as the United States, we explore who, exactly, should set priorities for a school, for a child. We delve into the consequences of an education system singularly focused on "college ready."

4. **The Ivory Tower:** College can be transformational for young adults, but its model is broken. We'll meet college leaders who are innovating in compelling ways and mavericks creating disruptive alternatives.

5. **Letting Go:** Parents want the very best for their child, but their actions can be counterproductive. Against their genetic instincts, they need to let their child explore, discover, fail, and find their own success.

6. **Social Equity:** In a country committed to opportunity for all, we give lip service to providing all children with an "equal education." In today's America, those who need the most get the least, and vice versa. This has dire consequences.

7. **Human Potential:** The purpose of school in our country today is to rank the potential of our children, not to develop it. Worse, we rank potential on inconsequential measures that offer outsized advantage to the affluent.

8. **Doing (Obsolete) Things Better:** For decades, U.S. education policy has centered on trying to eke out improvements from an antiquated model—"do things better." We'll understand why leaders gravitate to these policies and why these approaches are destined to fail.

9. **Doing Better Things:** We'll meet inspiring educators effecting change at scale with innovation change models. They understand that our schools need to "do better

things," not "do obsolete things better," and are establishing conditions conducive to real progress.

10. **It Takes a Village:** Innovation thrives when a community celebrates the aspirational goal of reimagining learning to elevate life prospects for its children.

Reflections: There are reasons to be optimistic that our country will transform its schools. If it's to happen, though, it will be driven by grassroots change.

Bear with me while I take a minute to describe this trip's challenges, mostly in a shameless appeal for sympathy. For starters, I travel simply. Strictly carry-on. Lots of Delta flights, National rental cars, and standard hotels. My sense of direction is abysmal, so I get lost a lot, even with GPS on my smartphone. My artificial left hip guarantees an obscene TSA pat down every darn time I go through airport security.

This trip was organized by Riverwood Strategies, experts in advance planning for campaigns. They rose to the challenge of squeezing the very most out of each day. For forty weeks, they arranged meetings from breakfast through late evenings, five and even six days each week. This took its toll—too little exercise and sleep, too much lousy food and considerable weight gained over the course of the trip. Oddly, though, I awoke each morning on an adrenaline high, thanks to a dose of daily inspiration from the teachers and students I was meeting.

Far and away the biggest hardship for me was being away from my family for nine months, apart from major holidays and an occasional weekend. My timing stunk, since the trip coincided with our daughter's senior year of high school. I made it to her graduation but missed most everything else. Trust me,

I'm fully aware that parents don't get do-overs for these precious years.

————— \\|// —————

You Really Need to Read This

From a thousand meetings during this trip, I'm sharing what blew me away, what I think you should hear. Instead of presenting stories chronologically, I've organized them into coherent chapters—the benefit of time to reflect after the trip.

When I report on something I observed, I use the font you see in this sentence, and I specify its location. Every story in this font occurred during this travel year.

When I offer my own perspective, I'll typically use this font.

Glossary of Abbreviations

CTE   career and technical education (a.k.a. vocational education)

ESSA   Every Student Succeeds Act of 2015, which shifted some education control to the states

MLTS   *Most Likely to Succeed*, a documentary directed by the acclaimed Greg Whiteley, which premiered at the prestigious Sundance Film Festival in 2015

NAEP   National Assessment of Educational Progress, the self-proclaimed national report card mandated by Congress that tests fourth-, eighth-, and twelfth-graders on math, reading, writing, and science

NCLB   No Child Left Behind Act of 2002, which escalated the role of standardized testing in our public schools

PEAK   purpose, essentials, agency, knowledge

RTTT   Race to the Top, a Federal initiative launched in 2009 to hold schools and teachers accountable to NCLB tests

STE(A)M   science, technology, engineering, (art), math

TFA   Teach for America, a program that recruits graduates of elite colleges, trains them for five weeks, and deploys them to challenging classrooms

What School
Could Be

Conventional Schools and Their Contexts

I used to consider myself an education expert. I had, after all, spent years in school as a student. What more is needed? My former expert-self carried certain assumptions, perhaps ones you share. Schoolchildren master fundamentals as they progress through proven curriculum. Test scores and grades tell us how much they are learning. A school's average test scores measure its quality. Children need to perform to rigorous academic standards, since life prospects hinge on a college degree. The more elite the college, the better the life. All this seemed evident.

The very first school I visited on this trip was quite conventional—not surprising since most U.S. schools are. Like all schools, it straddles two contexts—its nineteenth-century education model and its twenty-first-century dynamic world. One pulls it back in time, the other pulls it forward. In U.S. education today, the past is winning this tug-of-war. This school happens to be a high-performing suburban public high school. It could just as easily be a charter or private school. For reasons that will become clear, I'm giving it a fictitious name—Eisenhower High.

This school excels on every conventional metric. In the eyes of many, including my former expert-self, this school is the gold standard for American education.

Any Affluent Suburb, USA—As you approach Eisenhower High, you immediately recognize it as a high school—a sprawling two-story red-brick building surrounded by parking lots and expansive athletic facilities. A main entrance marked by flagpoles. An entry foyer lined with glass cabinets for sports trophies. Locker-filled corridors that oscillate between forty-five minutes of eerie quiet and three minutes of bedlam.

Comprehensive suburban schools like Eisenhower educate about half of America's 16 million high school students. Another 4.5 million go to urban high schools, many labeled "dropout factories." Some 3.5 million attend rural schools. A half million go to private high schools, mostly religious; a comparable amount go to charter high schools. A few hundred thousand homeschool. At least another million would be categorized as dropouts, although the number's elusive since many disappear from the system after middle school.

Eisenhower's students work hard, posting test scores consistently at the top of their state. Class sizes are reasonable, and teachers are articulate and knowledgeable. The principal is committed to the school's success. Eisenhower offers two dozen Advanced Placement (AP) courses, along with myriad after-school programs. All Eisenhower students graduate on time and go on to college, many to the Ivy League. Sports teams are a source of school pride, and athletic facilities are enviable. No metal detectors as you enter. By all traditional measures, this is a high-performing school.

When observing classes, I saw teachers imparting their domain expertise as they cover material. Students diligently take notes. Every so often, teachers pose questions to students, who raise their hands with answers retrieved from handouts or texts. Class participation affects their grade, so students are on their toes. Occasionally, a student asks a question of their teacher—invariably something like, "Will this be on the test?"

Administrators here wanted me to see their innovative practices. I visited two classrooms with students sitting in small groups instead of in rows of desks, although class discussion was controlled by the teacher. In a chemistry class, students were memorizing the periodic table with a "cool" iPad app. Their new community service program requires students to log twenty hours each year, choosing from three faculty-defined options. Student infractions are punished by adding more hours of required service.

I was able to meet informally with a group of seniors, all quite busy with classes, extracurriculars, and college applications. I asked why they come to school—"We have to," "To get into a good college," "To play on the football team," "To hang with my friends." Daily schedules were traditional—two were taking the exact classes I took my senior year forty-seven years ago. Regarding their studies, I asked which topics they found exciting. Blank stares, as though I was speaking a foreign language. Speaking of which, a few were taking Spanish IV but were at a loss when asked, "¿Por qué es importante estudiar una lengua extranjera?" When I inquired about interests pursued in their free time, silence punctuated by a few nervous giggles. No signs of absorbing hobbies, internships, projects, or jobs.

At the end of the session, one student lingered. He explained that Eisenhower's students feel pressure to get into the "right college." He described Adderall-assisted all-nighters cramming for tests. Many have SAT or ACT tutors, and feel stressed about their scores. He likened school to "being one of those hamsters on a wheel. We keep running faster and faster, but it doesn't feel like we're getting anywhere." As he was leaving, he remarked, "We know school is just the game we have to play. But, hey, we don't make up the rules. You do."

He's right. So what are these rules, and where do they come from?

To understand what rules the day at Eisenhower, or any standard school, we need to go back in time. Way back. To 1893, when education leaders anticipated that the U.S. economy would shift from agrarian to industrial. Farsightedly, they formed a Committee of Ten and proceeded to transform education from one-room schoolhouses to a standardized factory model. Teach students the same subjects, in the same way. Train them to perform routine tasks time-efficiently, without error or creative deviation. Produce a uniform workforce ready for lifetimes on the assembly line. The model worked, spectacularly. Over the course of the twentieth century, real U.S. per capita GDP soared from $3,500 to $23,000. A robust middle class emerged. Our nation rose to the top of every international measure of power.

This 1893 factory model was so successful that it remains with us to this day. Over the decades, an education infrastructure has grown up around it. This system, with its myriad interlocking parts, provides context to schools across America. If you aspire to being an informed citizen, you need to understand this context, dry as it might be.

- - - - -   \\|//   - - - - -

All Over, USA—Eisenhower operates in the context of governmental rules and regulations, governance bodies, financial constraints, and community expectations. And it sits amid a complicated web of other schools—the ones that feed it, the ones it competes with, and the colleges its seniors apply to. This context drives Eisenhower's daily regimen.

These graduating seniors have taken more standardized tests than any other students in their state's history. Annual state-mandated testing began in kindergarten. They've taken the PSAT, the SAT, and ACT (often multiple times), AP and SAT subject tests. Recently the PARCC assessment was added. Pick a few letters at random, and they probably took that test. Over their K–12 years, each student has taken more than one hundred standardized tests. The No Child Left Behind generation.

This school's community takes test scores seriously. They have no choice. The United States is a competitive society with a short attention span. Scores provide an efficient way to measure a person's aptitude, and a school's quality. So Eisenhower and its K–8 feeder schools train students to rip through questions like:

Math: Which of the following expressions is equivalent to $3*x^2 + 6*x - 24$

    a. $3*(x + 2)*(x - 4)$
    b. $3*(x - 2)*(x + 4)$
    c. $(3*x + 6)*(x - 12)$
    d. $(x - 6)*(x + 12)$

Verbal:

            POEM
       Some random poem
       About schedules and trains

       The kind of poem
       That dulls kids' brains

Dividing the poem into two stanzas allows the poet to:

    a. compare the speaker's schedule with the train's schedule
    b. ask questions to keep the reader guessing about what will happen
    c. contrast the speaker's feeling about weekends and Mondays
    d. incorporate reminders for the reader about where the action takes place

There's a recipe for excelling on these tests. Practice, practice, practice so you answer questions quickly, without thinking. Skip anything unfamiliar, rather than waste time trying to figure it out. Don't think creatively, since that costs time and points. Perform like a machine.

While there's no evidence that these tests have consequential predictive value or equip students with useful skills, they are widely accepted as the measure of learning, intelligence, and worth. Not exactly uplifting, but the stuff of these tests has become the stuff of our schools.

Eisenhower prides itself on producing "college-ready" graduates. Students, teachers, local businesses, and especially parents care about college. Every student goes on to a four-year college, with counselors and consultants guiding the way. Parents fight fiercely to give their child every college advantage. They see it as the key to their child's future and the defining marker of their parenting success.

The school's principal reports to a district superintendent, who in turn reports to the local school board. Superintendents have clout. Some encourage their schools to innovate; others push for better numbers (e.g., test scores, graduation rates, attendance). School boards hire, oversee, and at times fire their superintendent. Boards manage facilities, negotiate with subchapters of the state teachers' union, oversee budgets, and adopt policies and curriculum. Serving on a school board can require five to fifteen hours *each week*, making it hard to attract qualified members. Boards can make or break the success of a district and its children. Pay attention. During my trip, I asked top superintendents about the key to turning around a broken district. To a person they said, "The right school board."

Schools and districts interact with their state's Department of Education and its commissioner. Commissioners set goals and strategy, monitor progress, ensure governance, and advocate to the legislature for resources. During this travel year, I met with twenty-three commissioners—evenly divided between those more focused on policing schools and those prioritizing supporting schools.

Governors influence schools in their state. The dozen I met care particularly about workforce development. State legislatures specify standard-of-learning testing policies, curriculum, and the courses needed to graduate (typically algebra, history, and a science class).

State legislators generally aren't paid well (typically $35,000/year or less) and are required to be in the state capital during session (often several months a year), an enormous burden for those whose families and jobs are afar. I met some sixty of these legislators this year. They recognize that our education model isn't working, and some have supported legislation that encourages innovation. Few, though, have the time, staff, or passion to lead any charge.

Like all public schools in America, Eisenhower is funded by taxpayer dollars from federal, state, and local sources. Most federal dollars come from the U.S. Department of Education Title I program and the U.S. Department of Agriculture's "free and reduced lunch" program. While federal funds cover just 10% of national K–12 public school expenditures, they're deployed in ways to ensure compliance with federal regulations. A heavy stick.

The average school district in America gets 50% of its funds from its state, an amount trending down as budgets tighten. On average, 40% of funds come from local property taxes, with *enormous* variation. In most states, affluent districts have ample budgets ($20,000/student-year or more), while poor districts struggle ($10,000/student-year or less). Those who need the least get the most, and those who need the most get the least. Why? In the landmark 1953 *Brown v. Board of Education* Supreme Court decision, Chief Justice Earl Warren ruled that education "is a right which must be made available to all on equal terms." But a less-heralded 1973 Supreme Court decision, *San Antonio Independent School District v. Rodriguez*, drives inequity. Demetrio Rodriguez's children attended a poor school in San Antonio, while rich kids in adjacent neighborhoods were getting a better deal. He brought suit, but the U.S. Supreme Court ruled in a 5–4 decision that states aren't obligated to provide equal funding to schools. While *Brown v. Board of Education* promised America's children an education on "equal terms," *Rodriguez* makes clear that America is fine with vast disparities in *rich v. poor*. This matters.

The federal government played no role in education until 1965, when President Lyndon Johnson's War on Poverty included the Elementary and Secondary Education Act to fund programs for low-income and disabled children, bilingual education, and libraries and curriculum. In 1979, President Jimmy Carter created the U.S. Department of Education, which has grown to 4,400 employees administering a $68 billion annual budget. The 1984 Vocational and Technical Education Act provides modest funding of about $25 per student annually for career and technical education (CTE) programs.

In 2002 with bipartisan support, President George W. Bush signed into law the No Child Left Behind (NCLB) Act. It proclaimed that all U.S. children would be proficient by 2014, a patently ludicrous objective. Further, the act uses test scores as the sole measure of school "success." A school is a failure if even one child is left behind or if its students fail to post Adequate Yearly Progress on tests. Data hawks loved NCLB because it put testing at the center of education. Civil rights leaders loved it, believing that test scores would show that poor kids are getting shortchanged. Organizations selling tests, texts, curriculum, and test-prep materials salivated over prospects for more revenue—and unleashed their lobbyists to get this bill passed. The average citizen went along; who wants to leave a child behind? In 2009, the Obama administration doubled down on NCLB, offering waivers to states with subpar NCLB performance if they complied with Race to the Top (RTTT) accountability measures. Together, Bush and Obama made U.S. education the global leader in standardized testing.

In 2015, President Obama signed into law the Every Student Succeeds Act (ESSA), shifting some education control back to the states. Annual testing for grades 3–8 is still mandated, but states have more responsibility for test design and accountability. Under ESSA, states can obtain waivers allowing local performance- and competency-based standards. Obama commented, "One thing I never want to see happen is schools that are just teaching the test because then you're not learning about the world. . . . All you're learning about is how to fill out a little bubble on an exam and little tricks that you need to do in order to take a test and that's not going to make education interesting. . . . And young people do well in stuff that they're interested in. They're not going to do as well if it's boring." Truer words were never spoken, but they came late in his presidency.

Eisenhower High doesn't operate in a vacuum. No school does. It sits in a maze of local, state, and federal control, managed by officials often lacking classroom experience. Eisenhower is constantly compared to other schools on the basis of test scores, graduation rates, and college placements. A nearby expensive private school feeds its graduates into elite universities, pressuring Eisenhower. This state, like forty-two others, allows for charter schools. Here, charter schools focus on producing superior test scores, pushing Eisenhower to keep pace. It's generally agreed that this test-score competition is healthy. Schools in an adjacent low-income district emulate Eisenhower and its successful peers. As stakes rise for high schools, the community's K–8 schools are pressed to raise their game.

Eisenhower High reflects the reality and the aspirations of most of America's 130,000 schools—private, public, and charter. As Eisenhower High goes, so goes the nation.

A decade ago, I would have admired Eisenhower High. Their students excel on what our education system demands: committing content to short-term memory, sprinting from hoop to hoop, playing the game of school. We shouldn't criticize Eisenhower High's educators. They're conforming to the context imposed on them by an archaic system. This type of school made sense in the era of Dwight D. Eisenhower. Prepare young adults for an economy dominated by large, hierarchical organizations with employees performing to job descriptions. Equip students with citizenship skills suited to a democracy with trusted news sources informing us about civic-minded leaders. But Dwight D. Eisenhower died in 1969, taking a simpler era with him to his grave.

The students at Eisenhower High look good on paper. But their skill sets are useless in the innovation era, and they will be limited by their mind-sets. As toddlers, they brimmed with creativity, curiosity, and audacity. But these traits are gone, sacrificed in the crusade to produce transcripts that glimmer. These schools, these students, are the fool's gold of America's education system. They're museum artifacts in the innovation era, the context that will define the adult lives of these children. We need to understand it.

Vancouver, British Columbia—During my trip, I ventured briefly out of the United States to attend the annual TED Conference— the event where those famous TED talks come from. While there, I met with leading technologists to discuss the impact of machine intelligence on the future of our society. These people are the real deal—including chief technology officers of companies with global reach. They've spent decades helping create the digital economy through advances in machine intelligence—computer hardware, software, artificial intelligence, and robotics.

Before our meeting, a few of us chatted about the history of innovation and technology. While innovation is as old as civilization, its potential to transform society shifted dramatically in 1947 with the invention of the semiconductor transistor. This technology enables logic to be fabricated on dirt-cheap silicon and scale almost without limits. Gordon Moore, founder of Intel, predicted audaciously in 1965 that the raw compute power of silicon would increase exponentially for the foreseeable future. Six decades later,

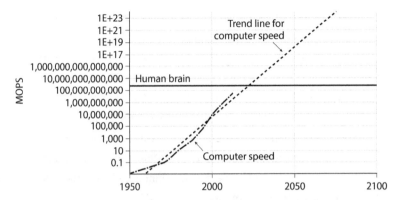

FIGURE 1.1. Race against the Machine. *Source*: Data from Mathspace.

his prediction still holds. Exponential growth is one of those high school math topics everyone studies but few ever use. In the context of innovation, it means that advances in the coming decade will be an order of magnitude more disruptive than since 2007, the year the smartphone's debut began reshaping society. Today's children will be adults in a world where the price-performance of machine intelligence is one hundred times as powerful as today. At least.

During our meeting, I asked the group if my message about innovation's accelerating impact is too alarmist. One pointed to our breakfast, predicting that within a decade most food we eat won't touch human hands in going from genesis to our tummies. Another observed, "Within twenty years, buildings the size of this sixty-story Fairmont luxury hotel will be 3D printed." Someone talked about a friend battling a rare and aggressive form of cancer; whose team of world-class oncologists referred his case to Watson, IBM's artificial intelligence software. A fourth shared a story about the founding team members at Google who bet their careers on being able to build the driverless car. When they started, the most optimistic believed it would take *at least twenty years* before autonomous vehicles would be road worthy. It happened in five years.

As the meeting wrapped, a few of us chatted about the future. Will technology's productivity turn society into utopia or dystopia? Hard to say without understanding a country's tax and education policies. What's crystal clear is that machine intelligence profoundly changes how, or even whether, an adult can contribute meaningfully to an employer or community. If nothing else, it's screaming, "Children need to learn to leverage machine intelligence, not replicate its capacity to perform low-level tasks!"

To bring this to life, let's speculate on what our typical day might look like down the road.

WHAT THE FUTURE COULD BE

You're connected 24/7 to vast resources through tiny devices on your watch, clothes, glasses, and body implants. No need to carry around a clunky smartphone. Your day starts with a made-to-order breakfast, compliments of your personal kitchen robot. Your virtual assistant briefs you as you eat. With a quick voice command, you summon a driverless car to take you to a meeting.

On your drive, you pass teams of agile robots maintaining your neighborhood—collecting trash, repairing buildings, tidying yards, policing for safety. A swarm of drones passes overhead to address an emergency. A corner lot, vacant just a week ago, now has a beautiful home manufactured by 3D printers, listed by an online real-estate site, and sold with the help of a virtual lawyer.

Your meeting includes a few people in person; most attend via lifelike holographic replicas. Each participant's virtual assistant tracks the conversation and provides relevant, curated observations in real time. Leveraging online resources, your group designs a complex initiative and implements it in a matter of days, for a few thousand dollars, and then continuously improves it with the help of big data.

Robots perform your errands. Your purchases are either 3D printed in your home or delivered in minutes by drones. To diagnose health challenges, you turn to artificial intelligence. An aging relative receives 24/7 care from an automated attendant. In your leisure time, virtual reality takes you to museums, cities, parks, or performances around the globe. The boundary between real and virtual life has blurred in ways that are uplifting, and disturbing.

This isn't science fiction. These advances are underway. We're heading into a world where machine intelligence excels in manual and cognitive tasks: a world stripped of the routine white- and blue-collar jobs that are the backbone of today's society. This is happening faster than we think, as automated solutions are already squeezing millions. Consider the Federal Reserve Board's data that 47% of adults in the United States can't pay an unanticipated bill of $400 unless they sell off personal possessions or beg money from friends or family.[1] Given the cost of a basic funeral, half of U.S. adults today are too broke to die. It stands to get worse. For these folks, the American Dream has turned into a waking nightmare.

If adults are competing with smart machines for jobs, they need distinctive and creative competencies—their own special something. But think about those students at Eisenhower High. They're

memorizing bucketsful of definitions, formulas, and low-level procedures. They're becoming proficient at low-level tasks handled
flawlessly by today's basic smartphone. They're being trained to
follow the rules. These kids are sitting ducks in the innovation era.

That our education system is failing is hardly late-breaking
news. Over three decades ago, the seminal *A Nation at Risk* report asserted,

> If an unfriendly foreign power had attempted to impose on
> America the mediocre educational performance that exists
> today, we might well have viewed it as an act of war.[2]

You might think that words like "act of war" would spur us to
think big, maybe form a bold modern-day Committee of Ten.
Nope. We thought small. Wring incremental gains from an archaic model through standardized curriculum and testing. Raise
the testing ante with No Child Left Behind. Double down on
accountability with Race to the Top. The result? Flat scores. No
change in the achievement gap. Bored, ill-prepared students. De-

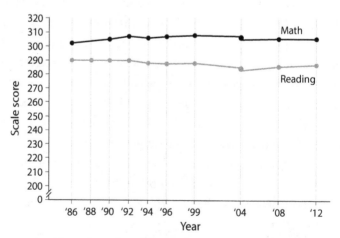

FIGURE 1.2. Three Decades of Flat Test Scores. *Source*: Data from National Center for Education Statistics.

moralized teachers. Focus on doing obsolete things better, not doing better things.

We're about to leave the land of conventional factory schools. But first, there's someone you need to meet. His story, his arc, speak volumes about education in America. Hear him out.

_____ \\|/_ _____

Stonington, Connecticut—He came up and said one short phrase: "February 6, 1992." I'm sure I looked puzzled as hell. After a pause, he repeated, "February 6, 1992." With most people, I would have promptly excused myself. But he didn't look like an oddball. Tall, prematurely gray, and patrician, he could be a governor or an ambassador. So I took the bait: "And . . . ?"

Doug Lyons explained that February 6, 1992, is the date when the *New York Times* first published international test-score rankings.[3] In a study designed by the Educational Testing Service, nine- and thirteen-year-olds in different countries were tested in math and science. South Korea and Taiwan dominated. American nine-year-olds were a respectable third out of ten countries in science but ninth in math. Our thirteen-year-olds ranked a dismal thirteenth out of fifteen in science and fourteenth in math. To rub salt in the wound, South Korea creamed us while spending far less per student.

The study explained that the rankings were suspect, largely due to differences in the student populations tested. But qualifying comments longer than *War and Peace* wouldn't matter. We're America, and our kids aren't at the bottom of anything. This was education's Sputnik moment. Given our hypercompetitive nature, we jumped into a standardized test race with both feet. February 6, 1992, marked the start of our educational *Groundhog Day*, repeating the cycle of mediocre test scores, collective angst over Asia's superior education system, fears of becoming a second-class nation, and doubling down on test preparation to close the gap. Nothing less than America's hegemony is at stake.

With a doctorate in education from Penn, Lyons has spent four decades in education. His first twenty years were in New Jersey's public school system as a teacher, coach, principal, and district superintendent. This "civil rights–era kid" was committed to public education, but plans changed. His district performed well on state-mandated tests—those tests whose scores get published in local newspapers. When an abutting district began closing the gap, "that made everyone nervous—parents and especially realtors—since part of what drives real-estate sales is the quality of the school system." The competing district, it turned out, was redirecting student time away from reading books. Instead, students were required to read hundreds of short passages and drill on the multiple-choice questions that populate our standardized tests—the passage's main idea, cause-and-effect relationships, signs of author bias, inferences, etc. Pressured to copy this program, Lyons quit. Even though this happened two decades ago, his sadness remains evident. "You know, my goal has always been to create lifelong readers—kids who love books, who feel a sense of loss when they've reached the end, who are moved, who cry."

Lyons moved to Connecticut to head a private school; in 2004, he became CEO of the Connecticut Association of Independent Schools. When it comes to school, he's seen it all. His side passion is the use of data in education. He cites Einstein: "Not everything that counts can be counted, and not everything that can be counted counts." But hard numbers inevitably crowd out qualitative nuance; people crave objective measures that facilitate comparison. Of many botched uses of data, correlations top the list, and Lyons challenges people to think through graphs like Figure 1.3. Thankfully, our country hasn't launched a massive mozzarella-eating campaign to produce more engineers. Yet we don't hesitate to push children to produce higher standardized test scores,

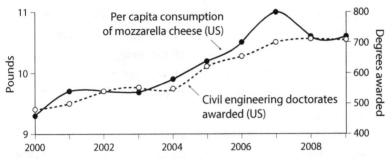

FIGURE 1.3. Spurious Correlations. *Source*: Data from National Center for Education Statistics.

despite no evidence that they're correlated to, let alone cause, anything consequential.

Lyons calls college admissions the "elephant in the room" that blocks high school innovation. "We know that the best education experiences are collaborative and social, where students are engaged and retain what they learn. But that is hard for a college to assess. They need us to rank-order kids." An Ivy League admissions director addressed his association, claiming they look for kids with diverse backgrounds, with real-world experience, with mundane summer jobs requiring hard work. Lyons pushed back, "We love everything you just said, but we know who you accept. You don't accept the kids you just described. You take the kids who go to SAT test-prep summer camps." Lyons is passionate about the need to "ratchet down the absurd expectations we have for young kids and eliminate family anxiety, even shame, over college acceptances." He notes that one-third of our kids in elite colleges are on antidepressants. "That's a disgrace. It becomes a forever thing." For our kids, "every achievement is a temporary high, which has to be followed by another achievement."

Lyons describes AP courses as "mountains of content minutiae— a Manhattan phonebook of trivia." He runs across many kids who work hard in AP, get a 4 or 5, and "never want to take another course in this subject again." He admires courageous schools willing to drop these standardized courses to challenge their students more authentically. He cites the work of the Independent Curricular Group or the Fieldston School, which replaced AP Biology with an Advanced Topics program where students collaborate via Skype with biologists around the world.

At the end of our conversation, Lyons observed, "We're in a uniquely exciting time. We understand how to engage kids. We need to give them real-world challenges, have them work with other kids, and provide them with the right kind of adult support. Project-based learning is how people work in the real world. We need to let our kids create portfolios of joy."

Real Gold amid Fool's Gold

Most communities have a local magazine that publishes annual school rankings tied to standardized test scores and AP courses. These lists make it easy to find schools like Eisenhower High, the fool's gold of American education. It's much harder to find real gold—places that engage kids and prepare them for their futures. In contemplating my trip, I hoped to find a few stellar examples, here and there. But that's not what happened. You're about to see a montage of purposeful learning, drawn from all across America. These stories grew to define my trip, and this book. We're about to see the real gold of education in America.

— — — — — ⋅\|/⋅ — — — — —

Fort Wayne, Indiana—At 6'3", 300 pounds, Jared Knipper could be an offensive lineman for the Indianapolis Colts. At a community forum, he raised his hand with a question. Given his size, I couldn't ignore him, even though he looked like he was going to say, "I think your views on school are a gigantic load of crap." But, microphone in hand, he explained:

> I was in the police force here for ten years. Four years ago, I left to teach kindergarten. But I didn't want to do what the state tells teachers to do. Even our pre-Ks here have rigid schedules and curriculum. I was lucky to have a supportive principal. So my kindergartners are designing robots, learning

how to use 3D printers, and making things. At the start, I didn't know anything about this and said to my kids, "Here's what you get to do, but you have to figure it out." One kid designed a prosthetic hand. It wasn't very good at first, but he kept at it. We're doing a big exhibition night in March, and the kids are on fire. I get pushback from some teachers and parents, but they're coming around. I guess I don't really have a question but would love for people to see what young kids can do if we just let them go.

As soon as the session was over, I made a beeline for him. I was blown away by the photos and videos he had on his smartphone. The prosthetic hand he referred to was complex, with multiple interlocking parts. Other projects were just as compelling. I wanted to know more.

Prior to teaching, Jared's police experience included serving at a local school as kind of a truant officer/assistant principal. While there, he saw bored kids learning little. Convinced he could make a difference as a teacher, he invested another fourteen months to get his teaching credential. He started as a substitute pre-K teacher but chafed against being managed to a rubric. He related, "I always had a vision of what I'd like to do with my own class, and it didn't look like what I saw around me."

In 2012, he jumped at the chance to teach kindergarten at Syracuse Elementary School. He wanted his class to be all about making things. Complicated, interesting things. No one—the kids, parents, other teachers, or Jared—knew what they were taking on. Some predicted disaster. But as Jared related, "Sometimes you have to just jump into the deep end and have confidence you can figure it out." Not to mention the courage to look ignorant in front of students. He adds, "One of the most satisfying experiences of my life has been learning right along with my kids."

I asked how his kids were doing on basic math and reading skills. He teaches math through "making." Children set up ten blocks, program their robot to take away six, and figure out how many blocks remain. Somehow, subtraction looks easy to a robot designer. To teach his students to read, Jared was supposed to adhere to ninety-minute uninterrupted blocks of time. He laughed. "I wish the people designing these schedules could show me a roomful of five- and six-year-olds who will sit still for ninety straight minutes." His kids are doing fine on reading, which Jared can't explain definitively. It could be that they're reading to figure out how to use the technology. It could be that learning complicated technical words helps them appreciate vocabulary. Or maybe it's just this simple: engaged kids learn rapidly across the board.

Near the end of the school year, they held an exhibition night, and three hundred people came to see these kindergarten projects. Some were "incredible" and some were "awful." Knipper's twenty-four students presented, along with others, as this initiative spread. Subsequently, parents, teachers, businesspeople, and kindergartners collaborated to fund-raise for more equipment. The community appreciated that these children were acquiring important skills from basic reading and math through to creative problem solving, collaboration, and figuring out complicated things. Knipper was giving these kids time to explore on their own, and they were rising to the occasion. Their learning has real purpose— like mastering what's required to produce a functioning prosthetic.

Knipper, who also coaches girls' softball, fits a pattern I saw across the country. Teachers with coaching experience prefer being the "guide on the side" to being the "sage on the stage." In reflecting on his teaching career, he related, "I see amazing people enter the profession, so I'm disappointed when I hear adults discourage someone from becoming a teacher. But I understand why. It's demoralizing to work in an environment that focuses on testing, where schools are reduced to letter grades, where teachers are micromanaged." Jared worries that his impact on his kids will fade when they go back to "sitting in rows" in later school years. But his coaching and police experience have shown him the importance of thinking independently, creating solutions, staring down failure. He knows what prepares his kindergartners for life. He ended by saying, "I hope I'm making a difference. I know what I remember from school. It's things I made and things I did for people. Hopefully, my kids will remember my class."

Sitka, Alaska—It was obvious as soon as I stepped into the room. Cindy Duncan, a teacher at Keet Gooshi Heen Elementary School in stunning Sitka, has second-graders doing extraordinary things. The room was chaotic, with kids clustered into small groups in loud discussions. Every child was engaged, their curiosity evident. It took me a few minutes to find Duncan, who was on the side listening to three children. Her website www.minecraftintheclassroom.com has the appropriate heading "Making Learning Irresistible."

Duncan's students are immersed in Minecraft as they design native villages or plan mining expeditions in the Klondike. She connects this to traditional activities like writing, historical research, and math. She complements Minecraft time with other forms of hands-on learning, including coding. While it might seem that all video games are a waste of kids' time, Minecraft actually is a "Turing complete" programming language. Her students support and critique each other's progress, and work frequently in teams. She uses Minecraft time strategically—a half hour on occasional school mornings. From the energy in the room, it's clear kids don't want to miss her class, which has translated into increased attendance and decreased tardiness.

When she started down this path, Duncan knew nothing about Minecraft, coding, or design. But along with her students, she dove in. She launched her program with support from her district. She regularly invites parents, educators, and community leaders to observe her classroom, helping spread this approach. Duncan poses this question to visitors: "Think to yourself—Are you more motivated to work on something you find enjoyable or interesting? For most of us, the answer is 'yes'—our achievement is driven by our interest. This is true even for children."

_____ \\|/ _____

Usually the more we do something, the better we get at it. But not with learning in school. Young children learn at warp speed. By high school, learning slows to a trickle. Ironic. As school gets more serious, students learn less. Given this, you'd think we'd try to make high school more like our early grades, but we're doing the opposite. During this trip, I saw very young children mastering impressive proficiencies, particularly around technology. They don't need to be taught. Given the right challenges and devices, they'll learn. These budding competencies can become decisive life advantages, equipping graduates to capitalize on machine intelligence. These kids in Fort Wayne and Sitka are off to promising starts. But if their upper grades ban technology in class and exams, we'll squander their potential to graduate ready to make the most of machine intelligence.

A quick aside on coding. It's trendy to assert that computer programming is a basic skill that everyone needs to master. That's just one of the inane statements that get tossed around education circles because it sounds good. In reality, a few brilliant coders write the software the rest of us can draw on. As machine intelligence advances, the number of coding jobs could actually decline. There will, though, be an explosion of opportunities for those who know how to leverage machine intelligence.

_____ \\|/ _____

Dunbar, West Virginia—Dunbar Intermediate School (DIS) is an elementary school, grades 3–5, in a relatively poor town outside Charleston, West Virginia. Upon first appearance, it seemed pretty typical, with things like hallway signs tied to its DIS acronym—"Determination Is Success." Jenny Spencer, the school's principal, has education in her blood; her mother is one of Kentucky's top educators. Spencer always knew she wanted to be a teacher and spent her formative years teaching early grades before moving into administration. After starting at Dunbar as interim head, she officially became its principal in 2014, itching to take on the challenges at a school with mostly blue-collar, low-income families.

Spencer wants "kids to love what they're doing so much they don't want to be anywhere else." Her students own their learning—they set goals, manage progress, and lead the discussion of how they're doing. "It's important that we allow them to go deep, to make mistakes, to explore. When you let go and engage the students, discipline issues disappear and real learning happens. When there's that buzz in the room." An issue at Dunbar had been that some parents historically weren't involved—either at school or at home—with their child's learning. That's changing as they focus on accomplishment, more than discipline and suspensions.

She related that when she first arrived at Dunbar, she'd ask students what they were doing. "They usually would tell me either 'I don't know' or 'I'm doing this worksheet.' I'd ask why, and they'd say, 'The teacher says I need to.'" Spencer offered an example of what's prevalent in our schools. A bored child leaves his desk to get a book. The teacher asks, "What are you doing?" The child responds, somewhat obviously, "Getting a book." The teacher asks sarcastically, "Did anyone give you permission to get up?" The student returns to his desk, humbled. Spencer noted that these examples are commonplace, and yet we wonder why students disengage from school.

Spencer has created roles at Dunbar that help students acquire essential skills while giving them a sense of purpose. Student Ambassadors conduct tours for visitors. Mine was a charming fourth-grader who described her school with pride and explained that her ambassador responsibilities had helped her overcome shyness. Later, I spent forty-five minutes with twenty Dunbar Technology Ambassadors. Like many West Virginia schools, Dunbar has received large technology grants. Spencer notes that tech can be "scary for teachers, requiring lots of training." So she gave this responsibility to the students, who are trained by the Apple Vanguard tech team. Students refine competencies while teachers get support for something otherwise frustrating. These third-, fourth-, and fifth-graders maintain SmartBoards, iPads, and AirPlay. They evaluate learning apps and understand the trade-offs. One walked me through several math applications, explaining how he helps classmates find the right resource. They use Periscope to explore what's going on all over the world. In advising and teaching classmates, they have to know their stuff. Spencer observed, "Kids can learn faster than adults. They don't need to be taught. We just need to let them learn." In addition to loving school and building essential skills, these young technology ambassadors are becoming so good at tech support that any local organization would—absent child labor laws—hire them.

Dunbar faculty used to give monthly awards to children for admirable behavior, with unintended adverse consequences. A kid polite to adults might win the compassion award, despite being a holy terror on the playground. Students lose confidence in their school when they feel it's not "fair." Her quick win? Students write notes when they observe admirable action, and the school celebrates successes each month. "They don't care if the same student keeps winning, as long as the process is fair."

Like most schools, Dunbar deals with occasional bullying. I was surprised at one manifestation—the quality of a child's shoes. Kids with new shoes make fun of those with scruffy hand-me-downs. When a bullied kid gets a new pair, they do the bullying. While at the school, I was standing up talking to the students. One of their Tech Ambassadors, Andrew, approached me to ask, "Would you be more comfortable if I got you a chair?" After bringing one, he then went and got me a glass of water. As we said our goodbyes, Andrew said to me, "Thank you for visiting with us. By the way, Mr. Dintersmith, you have nice shoes." Just a sweet, kind child who trusts us with his future.

In leading her school forward, Spencer has wholehearted support from her district superintendent. But innovation ruffles feathers. Spencer mentioned an anonymous letter from someone telling her, "You're giving these students too much power." But teachers there are energized, and she's effected substantial change in her school's teaching capabilities since arriving. She draws daily motivation from this conviction: "The poverty cycle will never stop unless we reimagine what we do with our kids in school."

Charleston, South Carolina—The emerging Charleston Collegiate School (CCS) is located in a community steeped in tradition—and stasis. This scrappy K–12 school makes the most of its resources. For example, they've turned a small plot of land into their school garden. Students take full responsibility for this endeavor, developing important life skills while elevating learning in biology, chemistry, math, economics, history, and literature. Headmaster Hacker Burr explains:

> We use the garden to teach kids that we all have our strengths and that good teams balance each other out with a variety of skill sets. We use it to connect students to nature, to teach responsibility. We use it to feed ourselves and serve our community by going farm-to-table at school and by taking excess produce to food banks. We use it to teach financial literacy as early as second and third grade in an unintimidating setting . . . with students harvesting things like cucumbers, learning the pickling process, discussing branding/pricing/

margins, and then going to the local farmers' market to get on-the-job training in sales and customer relations.

Innovation permeates CCS. Their outdoor education includes ropes courses, kayaking, and a mountain campus—helping kids learn to collaborate, welcome challenge, and face down failure. They've brought back shop class and industrial arts; brilliantly, their students are designing and building the new shop facility. They even innovate in making use of the school's core operations—facilities, event planning, marketing, kitchen, security, and finance. Each senior leads a team of a dozen underclassmen to help with a particular school function. Student teams support ongoing operations, and create and implement initiatives to improve things. In turn, support staff helps student-apprentices learn about a real-world operation. The adults can be effective mentors, able to relate to students comfortably since they aren't assigning grades.

Burr uses "surthrival" to describe how his school is doing. The early grades are thriving since families value an experiential approach for their young children. But high school remains a challenge, since families worry that colleges expect a traditional transcript. Burr reports one other source of pushback—kids who have "mastered the old way. They knew how to memorize and regurgitate. Now, we are asking them to grapple through things and use higher-order thinking skills." Mind-sets at CCS changed, though, once everyone "saw what they were capable of."

Every school has core operations handled by competent support staff. Few, though, tap these support functions to help students advance important life and academic skills. Consider students serving as apprentices to staff who maintain the school's buildings and grounds, plan expansions, and troubleshoot problems. These responsibilities draw on applied math, economics, ecology, engineering, science, and even history. Students could pitch in on the daily tasks that keep their school running, as well as take on challenges such as analyzing their school's energy usage and creating initiatives to reduce consumption. In helping "run" their school, students master hirable proficiencies and learn important life skills—like responsibility—through point-blank feedback from classmates and staff. Schools don't have to send kids on fancy trips to Africa to find opportunities to learn while making their world better. Just walk around your school or spend time with members of the support staff.

⁻ ⁻ ⁻ ⁻ ⁻   \|/⁻   ⁻ ⁻ ⁻ ⁻ ⁻

Fargo, North Dakota—Ben Franklin Middle School's eighth-grade history class decided to capture the stories of local historic buildings. Students established criteria for what constitutes "historic," researched buildings, interviewed adults, and wrote compelling narratives. One suggested telling each building's story with short videos and slide shows. Another suggested making signs for the buildings with QR codes, enabling passersby to use a smartphone to access student-produced videos describing the building's history. Another suggested organizing an event downtown, inviting the mayor, town council, chamber of commerce, and the greater Fargo community to see their work. With support from the school's entire teaching staff, these eighth-graders pulled this off.

In talking to teachers and students at Ben Franklin, it became clear that this project is transforming the school. Rather than memorizing historical facts, these kids are learning how to think like historians. History becomes fun, engaging, and relevant, drawing in other disciplines. Student work has real purpose as they gain essential skills. This small innovation—with lots of upside and little risk—is changing the culture. Early success sparks more teacher-led innovation. Last time I checked, the following year's class was hard at work producing a documentary for the Fargo Film Festival.

Innovation takes place in a context. Kirsten Baesler, North Dakota's visionary superintendent of public instruction, supports innovation in her state's schools. Fargo's impressive district superintendent, Jeffrey Schatz, is committed to preparing students for the twenty-first century. He works with EdLeader21, an organization helping districts bring clarity to "the profile of what competencies a graduate needs to be prepared for life in the twenty-first century." Fargo's profile calls for creative problem solving, critical analysis, collaboration, and communication. This North Star guides learning and innovation. When parents ask why their children are working on an interdisciplinary project, Schatz explains how the project work leads to the very competencies that the community holds to be essential.

One last North Dakota anecdote captures what happens to our kids in school. Kayla Delzer, a Fargo elementary schoolteacher, does amazing things with her second-graders. Among her innovations, she gives children unstructured time each week to run with their interests. She explains,

> The beauty of Genius Hour is that it allows me to really step out of the way. At the end of the hour, they will all be teachers because they are all going to teach all of us something they have learned. When you give your kids choice and make them responsible for their learning, test scores go up, engagement goes up, motivation goes up. Putting them in real-world situations where they're going to fail, well, that's ok, that's actually a good thing that we embrace.

A high school English teacher in Minot, North Dakota, heard about Delzer's Genius Hour and tried it with his juniors. He related that after informing them they'd have one class period a week to work on whatever they're interested in, half the students did a Google search for "What should I be interested in?" When I relate this anecdote to audiences, the initial laughter quickly turns to reflective silence. This is what we do to our children.

North Dakota is special for me. Odd, since the first time I set foot in the state was the summer of 2015, when I went to Fargo for my TEDx talk announcing plans to go to all fifty states. Almost instantly, volunteers in Fargo sprang into action to make North Dakota one of my first visits. A few weeks later, over five hundred people came to Fargo's historic downtown theater to watch *Most Likely to Succeed* and convene an hour-long discussion about school and its purpose. I was blown away by the energy of this town and its citizens. And North Dakota is where I started to see how pieces might fit together. The film *MLTS* energized the community. With EdLeader21's help, Fargo's schools have defined their profile of a graduate, their North Star. Schools like Ben Franklin Middle School and classrooms like Delzer's are taking small steps leading to big change, helping their students develop purpose, essential competencies, agency, and real knowledge. This struck me as the makings of a model for progress.

Reno, Nevada—Washoe County's Innovations High School (IHS), led by Taylor Harper, is part of the impressive Big Picture Learning (BPL) network of schools. Like the half dozen other BPL schools I visited this year, IHS is filled with kids excited about their in-school projects, advisories, and "leaving to learn" internships. One student who had served time in jail told me, "Being a scholar in a Big Picture school has shown me I can be anything in life. It also showed me that it's not really all about me. We can help the community and make it a better place." Another was called a "lost cause" at her prior school but has become a straight-A student with plans to study child development in college. A third talked about his twelve-week internship at the Reno Orthopedic Clinic and his goal of becoming a surgeon. Many IHS students were severely bullied at their prior school. One noted, "Coming to Innovations was the best decision I could have made. I do not miss the traditional, cruel, non-preparing school system, and I'm extremely grateful I decided to better my future, and my present, by attending a Big Picture high school."

Big Picture Learning aligns with the outstanding work of Brandon Busteed's Gallup education initiative. The 2014 Gallup-Purdue Index Report, titled "Great Jobs, Great Lives," analyzes the relationship between school and success later in life. They asked adults in their late twenties about happiness, employment, job satisfaction, and family status, along with questions about their education. They found that mentors, internships, clubs, and meaningful longer-term projects—far more than grades and test scores—were the pivotal preconditions for future success.

Andrew Frishman, BPL's co-CEO, joined me in Reno. Frishman often wears a suit and tie while carrying a briefcase and could readily pass as a high-powered corporate attorney. But that's not his path. His lifelong commitment to education and social equity got its start at age twelve, when he volunteered at a bilingual day-care center in impoverished Lawrence, Massachusetts. While in high school at prestigious Phillips Academy Andover, he continued to mentor kids in a Lawrence school. Separated by six miles, these schools are in different galaxies, a disparity he called "appalling." One has a 550-acre campus, two museums, stunning buildings and grounds, and outstanding faculty. The other is a decrepit building with bars on the windows, tattered textbooks, and overworked teachers.

Frishman earned his master's in education from Brown University, an experience that included a stint as an unconventional student-teacher at a high-performing school in Providence. For his biology course, he brought in medical professionals who dissected a brain for his class. His students had to contact and interview a neuroscientist. Everyone loved the course, except administrators concerned about protocol. Frustrated, he considered ditching his teaching plans when he happened upon a forum featuring innovative local schools. A student described a nearby school offering her internships, mentors, and the autonomy to pursue her interests. Frishman was on it like a dog on a pork chop and joined what was, at the time, one of two BPL schools. After years in the classroom, Frishman joined the parent organization and, in 2015, became BPL's co-CEO, helping them scale to schools across the country.

There's no better location in the world than Nevada, land of casinos, to observe the mistaken notions most adults have about probability and statistics—misconceptions that can be costly. Most people believe, for example, that a string of losses increases the likelihood of winning on the next play. So Nevada casinos are filled late at night with gamblers who pile up losses at slot machines, blackjack tables, and roulette wheels, convinced the odds are mounting in their favor. Such ill-conceived notions can lead us astray with life's most consequential decisions—large purchases, investments, medical decisions, career choices. In fact, almost every important life decision hinges on understanding probability and statistics. Almost none depends on algebra, trigonometry, geometry, or calculus—the backbone of grade 7–12 math. Go figure.

Grand Rapids and Adrian, Michigan—Grand Rapids, a community struggling with declines in manufacturing, is home to the ingenious Gone Boarding program. Bill Curtis teaches physical education in the Forest Hills Public School system and had seen too many kids drop out of school from boredom. While shooting the breeze with shop teacher Bruce Macartney, they brainstormed about how to keep students engaged. They talked about their own passions for making things, something kids love to do but that's largely disappeared from school. They asked students, "What would you like to build?" One thing led to another, and they created an in-school program where kids make boards—skateboards, longboards, snowboards, surfboards, paddleboards. Many schools would shoot down this idea, but their supportive principal said, "There will be obstacles. You may fail. But figure this out, and I'll take care of the naysayers."

Curtis and Macartney started with just fifteen kids and worked through numerous obstacles, including procuring equipment. They persevered and the program has taken off, spreading across Grand Rapids' high schools. Curtis noted, "For many kids, traditional school just chews them up and spits them out. They're bored and worn down. There's nothing in their school day they look forward to. This program changes everything. Kids conditioned to thinking of themselves as bad students, as dumb, discover that they have real talent. Now, our honors students, our star athletes, our cheerleaders look up to them and come to them for advice. It is transforming kids and the school culture."

Gone Boarding students learn math, physics, chemistry, and computer-aided design. They study the history of boarding and do related writing and reading—from fiction to technical manuals. They're immersed in teamwork, creative problem solving, iterating, and recovering from setbacks. Their work is held to high standards—a finished product used in the field and evaluated by teachers and classmates. Past students have gone on to interesting careers. Several now work for the world's leading snowboarding company, Burton Boards in Vermont. Two did a documentary on the program and have their own video production company. One group started their own board company in Grand Rapids. These kids are gaining expertise applicable to a range of careers—from auto body repair to a PhD in materials science—without textbooks, bubble tests, or scripted curriculum. Gone Boarding's slogan is "Dream It. Build It. Shred It." Their Shred Stories blog offers student perspectives like, "The lessons learned in my 'boarding' class apply more to life than anything I've ever learned in a math or science class." This initiative inspires students to dream and build, led by courageous educators willing to shred an outmoded education model.

Adrian, Michigan, 150 miles southeast of Grand Rapids, is another town hit hard by vanishing businesses. Over the past two decades, the high school's graduating class has declined from four hundred to two hundred. The town is full of pristine houses, well-attended lawns, civic pride . . . and empty storefronts. In Adrian, I met Gary Koppelman, who described himself as struggling in school and being told he wasn't cut out for college. But his guidance counselor believed in him and helped him realize he could learn, just not conventionally. He made it to college, did well, and found a passion for teaching. He's had a glorious career inspiring fifth-graders with an entirely experiential approach to science, and many have gone on to pursue STEM careers. He received the 2013 Shell National Science Teaching Award and has been honored at the White House. When we traded business cards, I saw an accolade that stopped me in my tracks—National Teachers Hall of Fame, 2014 inductee.

Gary's remarks at the Adrian community forum hit home. "Every school-day morning, I look at myself in the mirror and ask, 'Do I do what's best for my students today, or do I do what the state tells me to do?' " He talked about the damage done by testing and accountability in classrooms across his state. He spoke directly to the many young adults in the room planning on becoming teachers: "You're in this because of your passion for helping young kids. Don't let anyone dampen your commitment. These kids need you now more than ever."

Koppelman had me primed for my next morning's meeting at the State Capitol with several legislators. I was cautioned that attendance might be sparse, but twenty-five people came, including

Amanda Price, chair of Michigan's education committee. No one left early from what turned into a ninety-minute session. Representative Price had introduced a controversial bill requiring third-graders to pass a reading test or be held back. Tough medicine, and many parents in Michigan were anxious about its stressful impact on their young children. But I suspect Price has seen her share of high school kids reading at a third-grade level and wants to make sure all children are mastering basic reading skills.

During the meeting, I commented on the dismal life prospects for an adult lacking a high school diploma. Someone asked, "Should algebra be a graduation requirement?" I ticked off some standard algebra topics, asking questions like, "Has anyone here solved a simultaneous equation since high school?" "Defined and used a function?" "Used logarithms?" No one had used real algebra since school. I concluded: "Legislators decide what's required to graduate from high school. Many kids won't get their diploma because of a course most adults never use. If life goes south for them, you share the responsibility."

Austin, Texas—With the motto "Find a calling, change the world," Jeff and Laura Sandefer founded Acton Academy in 2008, with a goal of creating a scalable twenty-first-century model to provide children with superior, affordable education. Not for a few cherry-picked kids but for all kids. Acton challenges every core assumption of U.S. education, with far-reaching implications.

Acton is loosely organized into elementary, middle, and high school clusters—although the concept of grades isn't relevant at Acton. They push the concept of student-driven learning and personal agency to the extreme. Students set their own agenda, learn to access online resources, and manage their own progress. The school has no teachers, just a few adult "guides" who aren't expected to be subject-matter experts or allowed to answer questions.

When students need help, guides can only respond with relevant questions or suggested resources. Students organize their own Socratic seminars and create their "quests"—meaningful projects taken on individually or in teams.

For two hours, I observed two dozen eight- to eleven-year-olds immersed in their learning. During this time, not one adult set foot in the classroom. Let me say that again. A group of young children were left alone in a classroom and spent two straight hours learning—on laptops, in small groups at a whiteboard, or in vibrant discussion groups. At the end, I asked a few what they had been doing. Their explanations invariably started with, "Well, I want to understand . . ." or "The project I want to create is . . ." These classes run themselves—organically, a bit chaotically, but purposefully. Obviously, this isn't the case instantly with new students, but Jeff explained that most students rise to this challenge within a couple of months. How far does it go with Acton students? Unprompted at day's end, kids divided into groups to perform chores, including cleaning the school's bathrooms.

Assessment isn't swept under the rug at Acton schools. They believe in public exhibitions, group presentations, and student self-assessment—calibrated by adult review. Students update their progress on public charts. Children told me exactly where they stood against goals, what was going well, and what needed work. Mind you, I'm describing elementary school kids, not college students. The school uses standardized tests sparingly as diagnostic checks at the beginning and end of each school year. While tests aren't a priority, rates of improvement on test scores outstrip those of conventional schools, even though many students start at Acton with a history of testing poorly. In the trade-off between depth and breadth of content coverage, Jeff observes,

When young people want to learn, they learn at a 10× rate. So getting broad coverage isn't an issue. In Civilization, we make sure we touch all the important questions of history, economics, and politics, spread over time and many of the great heroes. In Writing, we have a broad selection of genres—far, far broader than traditional schools. The same for reading with Deep Books, life-changing books that usually have won a major prize or worldwide acclaim. In Math, we use Khan Academy. And our Quests rotate through the major sciences with real, hands-on work—plus subjects that most young people aren't exposed to until college or graduate school—like Big Data, Psychology, Physics, Negotiation, and Entrepreneurship.

The Sandefers aren't thinking small. From this flagship Austin school, Acton has spread to forty schools in thirteen states and seven countries. Currently, tuition is around $10,000, with many kids on scholarship. Their medium-term plan is to bring tuition below $5,000/student. As for what motivates them to take on this ambitious mission, Laura's response speaks for so many:

> The urgency I felt was very personal. I saw the light going out in my children's eyes when it came to school and learning. Jeff and I looked at each other and simply said, "No more. Let's create our own model based on what we know deep in our hearts." Today, the urgency is deeper because I see how desperately our world needs young people who know how to think deeply, communicate clearly, resolve conflict, and lead with empathy. These are the important outcomes I witness in the learners at Acton Academy every day. I truly am amazed by what young people—as young as six years old—can do when adults stop micromanaging them and give them space to think and grow.

_ _ _ _ _ \\|/ _ _ _ _ _

You've met inspiring educators doing exceptional things across the country, with modest budgets. You'll meet more. My intent isn't to overwhelm you but to underscore that there's no limit to what humans can create—art, inventions, learning experiences, or paths forward. Once you jump outside of the box, there's endless running room.

In observing great classrooms and schools, it was hard to see a forest amid many awesome trees. Each was outstanding, in its own way. Over time, though, patterns emerged—the advantage, I suppose, of full-bore cross-country immersion, with time to reflect. Across geographies, grades, school types, and socioeconomics, I came to appreciate that children thrive in learning environments that share four elements:

- **Purpose:** Students work on problems that are important to them and their community. They complete projects with real-world impact that can be displayed publicly. Over time, students gain conviction that they can make a difference in their world. Purposeful work builds purposeful students.
- **Essentials:** Like the Committee of Ten did over a century ago, these outstanding teachers understand the competencies and dispositions needed in the twenty-first century—creative problem solving, communication, collaboration, critical analysis, citizenship, and aspects of character. This profile serves as a North Star guiding classroom learning and innovation.
- **Agency:** Students have voice in their work. Starting at young ages, they learn to set their goals, manage their efforts, assess their progress, and persevere to completion. As they learn how to learn, they free themselves of the need for formal instruction. Personal agency can mean working at their own pace on a laptop, but it extends to their community as they teach, inspire, motivate, and learn from each other.

- **Knowledge:** Students master deep knowledge. They teach others. Their knowledge is reflected in the quality of what they create, build, make, and design. Guided by teachers, they acquire expertise on adjacent topics. While their growing body of knowledge is organic and un-predictable, their understanding is deep, retained, and held to a high standard.

FIGURE 2.1. PEAK Principles of Powerful Learning.

You saw these PEAK principles in the classrooms we just vis-ited. When we see them going forward, I'll note their presence by noting "PEAK." A school with a full-throated commitment to PEAK principles might look like this.

What School Could Be

Starting at an early age, children manage their learning. They take on ambitious projects that help them develop communication and reasoning skills, along with core reading and math proficiency. They pursue topics, create and build, and learn by doing. Assessment centers on demonstrated competencies, not memorized content. Standardized tests are used thoughtfully to identify and assist students lagging in "learning how to learn" skills. Students teach and learn from each other. They learn to make the most of online resources and machine intelligence and draw on adults for guidance. Students, and their teachers, have agency.

As students progress through school, their deepening competencies enable them to take on challenging initiatives outside of school's confines: internships, real-world projects, and deep intellectual exploration tapping experts around the globe. They learn to identify problems and opportunities in their community, create and implement solutions, and make their world better.

Students participate in regular seminars on greatness in the civilized and natural world. Seminar topics are fluid and dynamic, as students deeply explore topics of interest. Over time, students master the essentials of science, literature, history, math, and nature—in a powerful interdisciplinary way.

High school graduation requirements are based on demonstrated proficiencies, as well as completing an ambitious capstone project. Complementing their intellectual and artistic pursuits, high school graduates master competencies that give them an immediate high-skill career option. Graduates are self-directed young adults who can learn on their own, with economic flexibility and freedom.

The role of college in society has changed. It's required for certain credential-driven professions, and it can be transformational for those with deep academic interests or keen on expanding their horizons. College admissions is now based on authentic samples of student work, aligning "college-ready" with "life-ready." However, a growing number of young adults—from all socioeconomic and academic-achievement levels—now bypass traditional college. Adults of all ages accelerate their careers through periodic short-term immersive programs that broaden skills and interests, or simply by learning on their own. Many paths work in a world that values competencies and character, not credentials.

Emporia, Kansas—As my wife and I crossed Kansas, we spotted a highway sign for the National Teachers Hall of Fame (NTHoF). I'd heard of it from Gary Koppelman, the fifth-grade science teacher you met in Michigan. Stumbling upon it was a bonus. We exited, poked around, and found the museum and its outstanding executive director, Carol Strickland, a former inductee. Oddly, who should call Carol while I was there? Gary Koppelman.

The NTHoF inducts five new teachers each year after an extensive vetting process. To qualify, you need at least twenty years of classroom teaching experience, and you've inspired many students over many years. By museum standards, the NTHoF is tiny. It's a good-sized room on the Emporia College campus, along with a small chapel on a knoll memorializing teachers who gave their lives protecting their kids, mostly in the face of gun violence. One exhibit featured the T-shirt an inductee gives his science students, with "No Child Left Inside" printed on the front. Carol explained that the shirts reflect how he loves taking his kids outdoors to learn. An alternative explanation? "No Child Left Inside" reflects how NCLB eradicated the inquisitive, joyful child from our students.

We should be grateful that our country has a museum honoring teachers. However, its annual budget is tiny compared to museums honoring athletes or rock stars. The International Bowling Museum and Hall of Fame gets far more support and traffic. We're quick in America to express admiration for teachers, but we need to back that up in how we pay, trust, and honor them. If you come here, be sure to spend time on the knoll memorializing fallen teachers, including those at Sandy Hook, who took bullets to save their students. Then ask, "If we trust teachers with the lives of our children, shouldn't we trust them with a lesson plan?"

The role of teachers changes in PEAK environments. They don't try to outdo the Internet in delivering content. They empower students to find, critique, and leverage available resources. They don't lecture. These teachers advise, mentor, and coach. They care. They change lives.

Every school has teachers itching to create knock-your-socks-off learning experiences. In an environment of trust, they'll move forward and inspire those around them. As I traveled, though, teacher after teacher expressed dissatisfaction with available professional development resources—whether in college or in the field. To a person, they called for better ways to teach our teachers—the most direct path to modernizing our classrooms.

PEAK environments underscore a critical issue in education: trust. If we don't trust teachers and students, we won't have PEAK. Period. PEAK classrooms give students the agency to take unpredictable paths. No one can be sure what they're learning, nor does student work map neatly onto a traditional report card, college application, or standardized test. But remarkable things happen when kids learn organically and passionately, instead of painting by the numbers.

Prepared for What

In 1960, less than 10% of the U.S. adult population held a four-year college degree. College distinguished someone as being a cut above. Many of our country's most prominent figures were from powerful families with deep connections to elite universities (e.g., Kennedy, Roosevelt, Rockefeller). Phrases like "Harvard man" and "a product of Yale" became synonymous with superiority and success. The more society valued an elite university credential, the better these graduates did. College's own virtuous cycle.

Over time, college's cachet got baked into America's consciousness. I could serve up quotes and statistics, but I'll share a recent experience at a film festival. I was at a documentary about low-income African American students attending an inner-city high school that prides itself on getting all students into a four-year college. The school has an outstanding extracurricular program, which it holds over each student's head. Grind through your lackluster courses with satisfactory grades, or get booted from the program. At the film's conclusion, each graduating senior holds up the acceptance letter to the college they'll be attending. The audience went wild—cheers, tears, and a standing ovation. Of the long list of colleges, I had heard of only one. No mention in the film of issues like loan obligations, likelihood of graduating, or how much these students will learn. I broached concern to the person next to me, who responded ebulliently, "It doesn't matter. They're going to college!" That's America today.

With college at the top of our pecking order, our K–12 schools fall in line, striving to produce "college-ready" graduates. Affluent schools grease every skid, with students locked into an AP, SAT test prep, and extracurricular arms race. Low- and middle-income schools want the same opportunities for their kids and push their students along the same college-ready path. All schools—in overt and subtle ways—condition students to equate their worth with college outcomes, with parents piling on. College isn't just a goal for most students. It's *the* goal for *all* students.

When I was in high school, there was no college process. No test prep, no tutors, no obsessing over the perfect application, no sense of success or failure around the college process. But that 1970 world is gone. College admissions is a high-stakes, multibillion-dollar game. It's in the air and water of our high schools. And it comes at a price.

Baton Rouge, Louisiana—With time between meetings, I dropped in unannounced on Mentorship Academy. On a downtown walk, I saw a building with banners outside celebrating a school's technology programs. Intrigued, I rang the front-door buzzer and, shortly thereafter, an administrator kindly agreed to show me his school. Sort of.

By chance, I showed up at Mentorship on a "lockdown" day, when students were taking state-mandated standardized tests. I couldn't go near the students. They were, quite literally, locked in a second-floor room for their several-hour exam. My host explained, "No one, not even President Obama or Governor Edwards, can go inside without completing our state's test-monitoring certification program." Apparently government officials want to prevent the kind of cheating that took place in Atlanta, so they're going to extremes to ensure that kids can't access those darn resources they'll have at their fingertips for the rest of their adult lives.

Given it was a testing day, I didn't observe a typical school day for these 100% free-lunch students. I hope it emphasizes the compelling offerings celebrated on their banners—project-based learning, digital portfolios, robotics, 3D printing, and career-path exposure. It might, but one thing was crystal clear. This school measures its success by college outcomes for its students. No senior can graduate without getting at least two college acceptance letters. This school, like every other low-income school I visited this year, fills every square inch of hall space with college pennants and "College or Bust" posters. Day in and day out, these kids get the message: "You are a success only if you go to college."

- - - - -   \\|//   - - - - -

Prior to this trip, I brought *Most Likely to Succeed* to a high-performing high school. I won't mention its name, since they've had their share of press. The turnout for the event was stunning—1,500 parents, teachers, and students filling the auditorium and spilling into the gym. There was intense interest in alternative ways to educate children and help shape values. Why? The school has a history of student suicides that spike when students receive their SAT scores, early decision letters, and regular acceptance letters. For these students—children, really—college isn't an expensive, four-year commitment that should be analyzed carefully for how, or even whether, it is the right next step. College outcomes define these children, in their school and their family, in their lives and their early deaths.

Children should be encouraged to shoot for the stars, to dream big, to be supported by adults who believe in them. But college in America isn't a means to a dream. College is the dream. We don't tell kids to shoot for a star. We tell them to be a star student, to get good grades so they can get into the right college. And pity the child whose plans don't involve college. They'll get discouraging feedback from school, family, random adults, and prospective employers.

Education should prepare our children for life, but we have it backward. We prepare children's lives for education. It doesn't have to be this way. Let's visit places with the courage to break from the mold to help students find and reach their own definition of success.

\\|/

Cheyenne, Wyoming—In meeting with a dozen community leaders here, I learned that Wyoming is the only state in the country with the goal of preparing K–12 students to be "college, career, and military ready." Wyoming's values include deep respect for the armed services, not something front and center in some parts of the country. This departure from the norm sparked an interesting discussion. In a country as big and diverse as America, who should decide the purpose of school? Who should determine what we prepare children for? Who defines a child's success? Important questions.

Like other states, Wyoming's K–12 education system gets measured with "college-ready" criteria—college-focused standardized test scores, the percentage of students taking AP courses, the percentage going on to four-year colleges. But not on the basis of who could hit the ground running as a new recruit to our armed services. I shared with the group my running conversation with Robert Gates, two-time secretary of defense, who speaks articulately about our military's need for creative problem solvers. He describes Iraq and Afghanistan as the "captains' wars," where important decisions fall outside of the scope of policy manuals. The only generals he fired were those who couldn't innovate. I posed this question to these Wyomingites: What if the competencies that make a graduate "military ready" are the same that a Google or Facebook needs? Should we pay more attention to Robert Gates or to Bill Gates, whose goal is to "ensure that students graduate from high school ready to succeed in college"? That in the mix of "life ready," "career ready," "military ready," "citizenship ready," and "college ready," the odd man out is "college ready." Yet, bizarrely, the odd man rules the day in our K–12 schools.

Cheyenne's East High was a perfect complement to the morning's discussion. I met with students in the school's agriculture economics initiative, part of a CTE program spanning technology, planning and construction, computer programming, welding, culinary arts, business, and graphic design. Two young women raved about their agriculture class, complete with chickens, steers, pigs, tilapia, corn, and hay. They had set up a live webcast of a mother pig, following her through artificial insemination, pregnancy, and birthing cute little piglets. To their surprise, the webcast audience grew to sixteen thousand people worldwide. These students had thoughtful responses to my questions about farm-related math, economics, and biology. When I asked how they liked school, one said, "It depends on the day." They loved their "hands-on" days; otherwise, they'd rather stay home—a perspective they shared, somewhat fearlessly, with Wyoming's superintendent of public instruction, Jillian Balow. Neither student is planning on a career in agriculture—one was interested in law and one in physical therapy. Farming, though, is the hook that makes school engaging.

Governor Matt Mead makes his cell phone number public so that any Wyoming resident can reach him. Love these small states. Wyoming faces declining jobs and revenue, as oil prices have plunged. At a dinner at the governor's mansion, a few of us discussed a recent local newspaper article stating that the fossil fuel industry is far more strategic to Wyoming than wind energy. We talked about how schools like East High could take things to an even higher level, challenging students to invent, build, and maintain next-generation windmills. In a few short years, Wyoming could have the world's leading workforce in wind power—from technicians to PhDs—creating an economic future about minds, not mines.

Charlotte, North Carolina—Olympic High School in the Charlotte-Mecklenburg school district is a large, comprehensive public school drawing kids from mostly lower- and middle-income families. As soon as you walk in, you realize this is not your typical school. It's organized into five career academies:

- Biology, Health, and Public Administration
- Executive Leadership and Entrepreneurial Development
- Technology, Entrepreneurship, and Advanced Manufacturing
- Math, Engineering, Technology, and Science
- School of Arts and Technology

It's hard to imagine any teenager not interested in at least one. Ninth-graders choose an academy path but can switch later—unlike the German model where fourteen-year-olds get sorted for lifelong careers. I was struck by the respect given within these academies for a range of pursuits. Computer programming is on the same footing as welding. Ditto for biotechnology research and emergency medical training. Entrepreneurship and spreadsheet expertise. Nor did the school show any bias for college versus career. These kids are exploring different ways to plug into society as adults, based on expertise that gives them life advantage. All paths are respected.

Olympic has knock-your-socks-off partnerships with forty local businesses. You see the impact everywhere, including donated equipment and posters with job descriptions and starting salaries. Local partners regularly send personnel to the school to train, mentor, and inspire kids about careers. They offer internships and apprenticeships giving students an on-ramp into local jobs. Consider the following headlines from a recent school newsletter:

- Olympic Wins Microsoft "Spark Tank" Entrepreneurism Competition
- 8th House Built with Habitat Charlotte
- First Robotics with Partner Bosch Rexroth
- Mobile App Development Program with NAF
- Advanced Technology Manufacturing Center Launched
- Shark Tank Engineering Design Competition with Partner
- Operation Santa Claus Delivers Gifts to 1,000 Needy Children
- Developing 21st Century Workplace Skills with Partner
- K–8 Robotics
- Manufacturers' Apprenticeships
- Gaming Club
- Soft Skills Training
- Science Olympiad

One update from one school.

Olympic students graduate with a healthy balance of academic and hands-on skills. They can move forward in life with a job they enjoy, enabling them to support themselves and their family. They're learning how the world works. If they choose college over immediate entry to the workforce, they'll start with real-world experience and can defray costs with a high-paying part-time job. Seems like a gift for any K–12 graduate.

On a December Saturday morning, I met with a hundred of Charlotte's educators, parents, and policymakers, including State Representative Craig Horn and veteran teacher Carol Parrish. Horn's career is in the food services industry and Parrish teaches culinary arts. Over lunch, we talked about how cooking can be a window into broad, engaging education. Parrish's students read an "article of the day," underline sections of interest, circle unfamiliar words, and pose questions about the article. Her class draws kids into math, economics, chemistry, biology, literature, and history. She gets her students excited and builds from there. PEAK. Her approach resonated with Horn, a busy legislator giving up a Saturday morning to learn more about helping his state's kids. But he has his hands full. Under former governor Jim Hunt, North Carolina was an emerging national leader in education. Now, its system is falling apart. They've cut teachers' salaries to the point where many in Charlotte drive an hour each way for a teaching job in South Carolina.

Albuquerque, New Mexico—In a city with deep poverty, Tony Monfiletto works tirelessly to advance life prospects for Albuquerque's poorest kids. Years ago, he started a successful college-prep high school but came to realize that "it was very academic, preparing young people for college. That framework didn't serve a lot of our young people who need an applied learning experience. That academic pathway was leaving many young people behind, which is so hard on the community." So Monfiletto took a sabbatical to reimagine high school for his community. Convinced of the potential of project-based learning, he founded the New Mexico Center for School Leadership to incubate new schools. It's already launched the ACE (Architecture, Construction, and Engineering) Leadership High School, the Health Leadership High School, and Siembra Leadership High School, all free public charter schools working with students otherwise unlikely to graduate. The city of Albuquerque has a 40% dropout rate, so there's no shortage of prospects.

Monfiletto explains that these schools "plan backward from what our industry partners need. We have industry people pitch ideas to our schools, and teachers partner with them to create projects." He adds:

When you start working with young people to meet their social and emotional needs, you realize the instruction you've got isn't adequate. Drill and kill so they can take a test successfully becomes less meaningful because you've uncovered what they really need—to be engaged with adults and their own learning. Once you start acknowledging the unique needs of young people, you realize how flawed the system is.

One partner is the Albuquerque Sol, a minor league soccer team that aspires to major league status. To grow support, they want to make more effective use of social media to reach fans, especially younger next-generation supporters. Tony relates, "We realized there was a partnership waiting to happen . . . since young people are experts in social media." Siembra's student teams—mainly in-poverty Hispanic kids who floundered in traditional school—are crafting and implementing campaigns to help the Sol leverage Facebook, Twitter, and other fast-changing options that adults aren't clued in on. Sol takes the project seriously, investing resources to implement student-driven strategies. As Tony notes, this project is "real, there's a real client, there are real stakes involved."

So fast-forward. This project engages students as they learn essential skills. They're getting good at writing, graphic design, and applied math. They're becoming experts in an area they find fascinating, which happens to be a hirable skill needed by any organization. PEAK. But here's the shocker. In visiting two hundred schools across the country, this is the *only* example I found of kids developing social media expertise applied to real-world challenges.

Let's use some estimation math to gauge this project's impact. A social-media expert with references can charge at least $30/hour for their services. With this expertise, a student can earn about $20,000 in a year, working fifteen hours per week during the school year and full-time during the summer. During high school, they can build up savings. If they go to an in-state college, they can cover all costs. If they make this their full-time job, they can earn $40,000 or more annually. Since they can add value to almost any employer, they can get their foot in the door of any company they find interesting and shape their career path accordingly.

These kids in Albuquerque underscore what's at stake in U.S. education. Left in a standard school, these kids would drop out, facing grim prospects. Now, they are taking on compelling real-world challenges, are building skills that launch them into intellectually challenging careers, will graduate able to support themselves and their family, and are contributing to their community. School is empowering these kids, not failing them.

The testing and accountability policies of New Mexico's secretary of education, Hanna Skandera, are controversial here. I found her to be informed and committed to education. But as I traveled across the state, the teachers I met were professional, dedicated . . . and anguished. One, in tears, described what it's like not to be trusted. At a Santa Fe community forum, a teacher described to a district superintendent how any deviation from tightly prescribed curriculum results in a reprimand from the principal. The superintendent advised her, "Well, you'll have to work with your principal." I jumped in, telling him that if he doesn't stand up for innovation in the classroom, it won't happen, and New Mexico's children will bear the consequences.

Helena, Montana—"Helena," Governor Steve Bullock explained, "used to have more per capita millionaires than any other city in the country." In the late nineteenth century, some fifty residents of this tiny town were millionaires, extracting fortunes from nearby gold mines. With a total population of just under 30,000, Helena today is the fifth smallest U.S. capital (behind Montpelier, Pierre, Augusta, and Frankfort). While it was hardly a trip goal, I ended up visiting nine of the ten smallest capitals, only missing #9, Jefferson City.

Bullock is a champion for linking school to real-world careers and serves on the board of Jobs for America's Graduates. With its sparse population, his state doesn't have the luxury of creating many new schools. It's one of seven states without charter schools, something I've come to view as advantageous after seeing such deep divisions between charter and mainstream public schools in many states. With a total population of just one million, Montana has 440 school districts, compared to Florida's 67 and Hawai'i's 1. The average Montana school district has just 320 students.

Stephanie Thennis started her career running marketing for a minor league baseball team and rose to become general manager of the Helena Brewers. When the team moved out of state, she stayed in Montana to pursue her dream job of teaching marketing to high school students. Later in her career, she became principal at Helena's PAL (Project for Alternative Learning) High School, an alternative school mostly for kids who dropped out of their mainstream school because of boredom, a need to earn money, a learning style not aligned with conventional school, early pregnancy, or some form of trauma. While PAL's building is no-frills, its students are energized by their opportunities for job shadowing, internships, and career pathways in fields like automotive, welding, clothing/fashion, woodworking, and information technology. One student there absolutely hated school but loved restoring old cars. He's thrived at PAL, where they leveraged his passion for cars to spark interest in science, math, history, and literature.

About 80% of PAL students graduate, impressive given their academic history. To get their diploma, they must meet the state's required coursework in English, government, science, and algebra. PAL offers a math-intensive course in financial literacy, but it doesn't count for math credit since it's taught by a CTE teacher. Algebra does, though, since it's taught by someone with proper math accreditation. Just one of those bullshit things you find under every education rock. Thennis lit up describing her students' marketing

projects—creating a fund-raising event for a local charity, designing a campaign for a local business, and forming teams that compete to sell more of a product. Her students get good at public
speaking, accounting and math, writing, and web design—skills
that open career doors.

Jackson, Mississippi—On every education metric, Mississippi struggles. Whether on graduation rates, college matriculations, National
Assessment of Educational Progress (NAEP) scores, SATs, or ACTs,
the state's rank is a two-digit number starting with a 4 or a 5. Governor Phil Bryant is on this. Born and raised in Mississippi, Bryant is
the son of a diesel mechanic. Dyslexic, he struggled in school and
readily admits how little he got out of classroom time. He viewed
school as something "you had to put your time in on, while looking forward to getting away from it. It should have been the opposite." He attributes out-of-school experiences—even something
like building a tree house—for helping him hone creative problem-
solving skills.

When asked about his most memorable learning in school, he
recalls skipping a tenth-grade biology class to play pickup football
outside, where he saw and caught a big snake. He brought it into
the school, knocked on the door to his biology class, and thrust
it into the room. He howled, recalling how students fainted or
hid behind desks. The beating he got from his football coach,
Mr. Withers, was his most memorable school learning experience.
"I learned never to bring a snake into school again."

Bryant went on to community college and later got his undergraduate degree from the University of Southern Mississippi and
an MS from Mississippi College. He's served his state in elected positions, as well as teaching political history. During his school years,
he notes, "I was never a math guy," but notes, "I could tell you all
you wanted to know about a 283 cubic-inch engine, its firing order,
and how many horsepower it could deliver." As state auditor for

eleven years, Bryant relates, "all it required was adding columns." I asked about math requirements for a high school degree in Mississippi. Students need to pass Algebra I and II, which I urged him to rethink.

Bryant has three guiding principles for his education work: "Immerse yourself in the issues. Be brutally honest about what is and isn't working. Offer solutions." When he took office, he mortified the education establishment by calling the state's education system "abysmal. But we needed to face reality." Bryant pushed into law a bill requiring all kids to pass a reading proficiency test at the end of third grade or be held back. No exceptions. He explained, "I'm tired of schools passing kids from grade to grade without equipping them with the single most important skill needed to learn: reading. We have high school students here reading at the third-grade level. That's shortchanging these kids, and I'm putting an end to it." Maybe there's a less draconian approach, but it's hard to fault this objective.

In a debate about whether the purpose of school is something lofty or pragmatic, Bryant is clear. Mississippi's poverty lends credence to his practical bent. He chairs Jobs for America's Graduates (JAG), an organization formed in 1980 with the goal of boosting high school graduation rates and equipping graduates with skills for productive careers. It now reaches more than 1,250 school communities and 57,000 students across 35 states. Since inception, JAG has helped more than 1.1 million students. As a national cohort, JAG's 2016 graduates posted stunning results for at-risk kids. Some 95% graduated, and 84% moved successfully to employment, the military, or higher education. Full-time job placement rates were triple the national average for this population of kids. A survey conducted by the U.S. Chamber of Commerce found off-the-charts rankings by employers of JAG students and graduates.[4] Going forward, JAG is working with the Buck Institute, a leader in project-based learning, to bring even more compelling learning experiences to its schools. JAG's scalable impact is a big deal as they work to ensure that every student, irrespective of socioeconomic level, can reach a rung on the economic ladder.

Our national K–12 education mantra is "College and Career Ready," but the phrase is misleading. In reality, schools prepare students for their college application, not college. Career is strictly an afterthought. In fact, most schools have eliminated anything practical, like shop, to make more time for college-ready courses. A small fraction of high schools offer "career-ready" CTE programs, and we just visited a few with excellent teachers, engaged students, and learning connecting the practical to the academic. However, CTE programs generally struggle for funding, are limited in scope, and fight the perception of being a last-resort option for "those kids" who can't cut it academically.

CTE education deserves more emphasis, and respect, in our schools. During the year, I observed a workshop with a group of district superintendents. At one point, they reviewed a student's essay laying out recommendations to a Bangladeshi community about earthquake preparation. These educators were asked to evaluate the essay on the basis of creative problem solving. Most gave it high marks. The essay presented factual content eloquently but lacked any substance. In the ensuing discussion, these superintendents explored their potential bias for academia's style over real-world insight. With lives at stake, they'd rely on informed advice from a CTE student with construction expertise, not flowery prose from an AP English star. Yet in the hierarchy of school, it's the AP student who is viewed as gifted.

High school could combine the academic and the applied. Chemistry and culinary: physics and wiring electrical systems: history and producing documentaries: civics and legal defense casework. Give students credit for real-world projects and internships. Support students who go deep into a discipline to create a fulfilling career path. These environments would give non-academic students opportunities to shine, broadening everyone's perception of intelligence. High school graduates could gain financial independence, irrespective of college plans. But that's not the world of our students. They study material they don't care about, won't retain, and won't use later in life. Consider these. The quadratic equation. Iambic pentameter. The periodic table. The Progressive Era. Foreign vocabulary words. Newton's Laws. Diagramming sentences. Factoring polynomials. State capitals. Avogadro's number. Gerunds. Dissecting an earthworm. And on and on. These phrases take you right back to high school, the last time they were in your life.

We rationalize our curriculum by waving our hands. "They're learning the fundamentals" or "We're teaching them to think" or "They're building grit." Here's the reality. This curriculum pervades our upper grades for one simple reason. It prepares students for the college-ready tests demanded by admissions officers and state legislators.

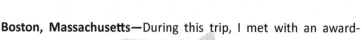

Boston, Massachusetts—During this trip, I met with an award-winning national journalist researching Common Core. She's a Yale graduate with a lifelong passion for Victorian literature. As background research, she took the tenth-grade English Language Arts/ Literacy test administered by the Partnership for Assessment of Readiness for College and Career. It appeared she caught a break when her reading passage was a fictional piece set in nineteenth-century England—right up her alley. She expected a high score but got a disappointing 79. She talked about the obvious influence of literature PhDs in selecting a formal, archaic passage—something alien to many high school kids. Her composition might well have been graded by someone hired recently off of Craigslist, compensated for how many essays they grade each hour. Should the typical tenth-grader perform better than an award-winning journalist? Should we hold teachers accountable to these tests? Should we be surprised if our classrooms focus on test-taking tactics, not real learning?

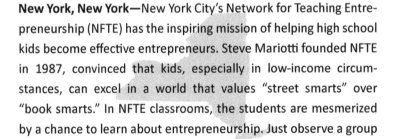

If a goal of education is to get students excited about literature's great works, an essential question is how to spark such passion. Should we require students to read classics and expect fervor to erupt? Make teenagers read *King Lear* and expect them to love a piece that Shakespeare intended audiences to see, not read? Or, do we seek to foster a love for language through whatever hook works for a child—Harry Potter, slam poetry, Emily Brontë, or rap? And build from there. Far too often, our well-intentioned efforts backfire, and assignments actually turn kids off to the greatness of nature and human accomplishment.

New York, New York—New York City's Network for Teaching Entrepreneurship (NFTE) has the inspiring mission of helping high school kids become effective entrepreneurs. Steve Mariotti founded NFTE in 1987, convinced that kids, especially in low-income circumstances, can excel in a world that values "street smarts" over "book smarts." In NFTE classrooms, the students are mesmerized by a chance to learn about entrepreneurship. Just observe a group of high school kids watching *Shark Tank*. To date, NFTE has reached more than 700,000 kids in 23 locations and 10 different countries.

A NFTE highlight is their annual business competition. Students identify opportunities, perform market research, create a business, and generate product sales. They present their work to an audience, responding to tough questions from experts. Their presentations can be recorded and archived in a digital portfolio that can be shared with potential employers, or even colleges admissions offices willing to review authentic work. NFTE students build essential competencies while being rewarded for resourcefulness and determination. In constructing a business plan, they improve their reading, writing, and math skills. They're more likely to graduate, and they enter adulthood with a distinctive edge in getting or creating an interesting job. PEAK.

The topic of summer comes up regularly in education, often in the context of how much students regress during these three months. Imagine students who develop hirable skills during the school year and then market their expertise during the summer. Such entrepreneurial experience would equip them with the skill sets and mind-sets to be off and running in a world of innovation. But in the world of conventional education, summer is the lost season. Students forget what they've "learned" and dread returning to school where they'll push short-term memorization boulders back up the hill.

In today's world, everyone needs to be entrepreneurial. Not entrepreneurial in the sense of starting a for-profit business but in the sense of fighting tirelessly to improve your world through your skills, passions, perseverance, audacity, and community support. It's the essence of our humanity—to create, to invent, to make our world better. Giving students and teachers the support and permission to be creative and entrepreneurial isn't optional in the twenty-first century—it's indispensable.

In serving on the NFTE Board several years ago, I came to appreciate the challenges of securing funding from large foundations demanding hard data on impact. NFTE faced constant pressure to prove its effectiveness. Complicating things, funders wanted proof that NFTE helps students be more entrepreneurial. Random audits of student work apparently weren't adequate, nor were indirect measures showing increased attendance and graduation rates.

I was thrilled to participate in NFTE's annual meeting, with its theme of the "entrepreneurial mind-set." The meeting included a session on the age-old bugaboo of measurement, and a leading test services organization pitched a standardized-testing approach to measuring "entrepreneurial mind-set." If this becomes reality, I can only imagine the test questions they'll come up with:

1. The word "entrepreneur" became commonplace in the English language in:
   a. 1849
   b. 1922
   c. 1958
   d. 1999

2. Which is least germane to an entrepreneurial mind-set?
   a. resilience
   b. leadership
   c. ability to write a sound business plan
   d. failing

3. If it takes two entrepreneurs fifteen months to start a business, how many months will it take seven entrepreneurs, assuming the five new team members are two-thirds as productive as the original two?
   a. 30 months
   b. 5.625 months
   c. $\cos(2\emptyset)*\pi*e^i$
   d. who cares and why are you asking this?

My two cents' worth? The people designing our standardized tests ought to answer the following question before asking for hundreds of thousands of dollars to design an entrepreneurial mind-set bubble test:

4. A public exhibition of entrepreneurial projects completed by students is:
   a. an informed twenty-first-century assessment
   b. motivating for the student
   c. consistent with how employers will evaluate the work of employees
   d. a threat to the long-term revenue of ETS and the College Board
   e. all of the above

Minneapolis, Minnesota—Jon Bacal, a Minneapolis education entrepreneur, founded Venture Academy for students growing up in deep poverty. In a brainstorming session, we talked about the role of entrepreneurship in education and then turned to what kids could pull off in a school willing to ignore "college ready." We hardly broke a sweat coming up with immersive experiences kids love and that lead to interesting careers. They asked me for salary levels for young adults adept at skills such as video production, social media optimization, 3D modeling, data analytics, algorithm structuring, design thinking, music composition and sound editing, graphic design, copywriting, or computer programming. I estimated that young adults with these proficiencies could earn at least twice the minimum wage. Jon observed, "That's more than any parent here makes today." We noted the irony that high school students learn what's needed to get into college, so they can spend four years and $100,000 or more for a college degree, which might, just might, lead to a satisfying job. Yet most schools with lower test scores want to catch up to schools with higher test scores, rather than just flat-out leapfrogging them.

Bacal organized a dinner with a dozen influential leaders in Minnesota education. During a spirited discussion, one person staunchly defended the primacy of content. This chemical engineer asserted, "Everyone needs to memorize the periodic table." Yet no one else at the table could recall a single time they needed this information since their chemistry class. A few minutes later, she politely excused herself and departed. That very day, David Brooks devoted his *New York Times'* column to *Most Likely to Succeed*. He began with: "Friends of mine have been raving about the documentary *Most Likely to Succeed*, and it's easy to see what the excitement is about." But Brooks took issue with high school kids learning by doing, arguing that the path to higher-order skills requires years of "basic factual acquisition. You have to know what a neutron or a gene is, that the Civil War came before the Progressive Era." But how many adults can really explain neutrons, genes, or the Progressive Era? Can you? Content covered is not content retained.

So we find ourselves staring at the twin orbiting black holes that suck the joy and learning out of our K–12 schools: expansive college-ready content coupled to high-stakes standardized tests.

College-ready content in our schools has grown like kudzu, with AP courses leading the charge. As students work harder to cover ever more content, it's tempting to conclude they're learning more than ever. But consider Lawrenceville Academy, one of our nation's elite private schools. Highly selective and expensive ($61,240 annually for boarding students), this school's outstanding faculty teaches some of our nation's highest-performing students, who then go on to our most elite colleges. A few years ago, Lawrenceville conducted an important experiment, something all schools should replicate. Students returning in September retook their final exams from three months earlier. To be precise, faculty removed low-level material they didn't expect students to retain over the summer. On tests of just the essential concepts, the average grade fell from a B+ to an F. Lawrenceville conducted this experiment for two years, with many students and several subjects. Not one student retained all of the essential concepts that the school expected every student to have mastered. This raises a vital question. Are even our highest-achieving students really learning?

Think of an expertise you've mastered. Would it disappear entirely in a few months? When it comes to evaluating student accomplishment, there's a world of difference between informed assessment and standardized testing. A domain expert can assess a student's essay, a play, a science experiment, or an entrepreneurial venture. They can offer constructive criticism, feedback, and an evaluation based on direct evidence. Standardized tests are a totally different ball game. Administered to the masses spread around the globe, they rank a student's performance to the exact percentile. Typically, they are designed to produce a bell curve (or *standardized* curve) of results, meaning only small tails of the tested population get outstanding or dismal scores, with most test takers slotted for mediocrity. To facilitate inexpensive computer-driven scoring, multiple-choice questions with a "right" answer are the staple.

Standardized tests can evaluate low-level reading and math capabilities, helping ensure that children are "learning how to learn." But bulk tests don't lend themselves to higher-order competencies like creativity, communication, critical analysis, collaboration, leadership, tenacity, and entrepreneurship. We can't rank someone's leadership precisely at the 93.7th percentile. It's silly to try to score one person's tenacity at 742 and another's at 515. Try as they might, bureaucrats can't determine that the average creativity score for a district in Phoenix is at the 55.6% level while a Dayton district comes in at 54.2%.

Across America, our kids study what's easy to test, not what's important to learn. It's easy to test factual content and low-level procedures, so that defines the curriculum. It brings to mind a joke about a drunk trying to find his car keys under a streetlight.

A helpful stranger stops to ask, "So where do you think you lost your keys?" The drunk responds, "A few blocks back." "So why are you looking here?" "Well, this is where I can see." We'd all agree that the drunk is wasting his time, but what about our students? The next time you hear an education policymaker say, "We have to be able to measure it," think of the drunk under the streetlight. Those eight words do untold damage to the futures of our children.

Chicago, Illinois—Jim Nondorf understands college admissions and its impact on lives. Educated at Yale, he accomplished his business goals early and returned to his alma mater to work in its development office. In raising money for an outreach program, he was drawn to opening doors for kids in tough circumstances. He moved into admissions there, thrived, and in 2009 became dean of admissions at the University of Chicago. This passion led to his chairing the Coalition for Access, Affordability, and Success, an initiative with the potential to influence education across America.

Nondorf regularly deals with parents anxious about their child's college prospects. He reassures them that "it's OK if your child didn't build a hospital in Nicaragua." He looks to distinguish between a genuinely motivated kid and a parent-driven child "just along for the ride." Nondorf notes, "Admissions isn't a scorecard. It's not a matter of doing these eight things, and then you'll get the outcome you want." His worst experience? A father called to contest his son's rejection, explaining, "I can't let this go. This would be the first time I've not been able to give him something he wants."

In the world of college admissions, the Common Application rules the day. It centers on academic numbers (GPA, ACT, SAT, AP, class rank), lists of extracurriculars, and generic essays. Rich families go after these criteria with a vengeance, supporting their kids with college prep materials, tutors, and college counselors. Poor families struggle to keep up. All kids are pushed to excel on measures that are tailored to the priorities of admissions officers and testing organizations.

In 2013, the Common App experienced what was called "a glitch-ridden nightmare." Captive to a single vendor, a few leading admissions officers began exploring an alternative and realized they could do better. Thus began the Coalition for Access. Endorsed by over one hundred respected public and private colleges, the coalition offers an application platform, a digital locker for student work, and online access to guidance counselors, mentors, and alums. Students can select samples from their digital portfolio in constructing an application that reflects their progress, creativity, and authentic achievement.

Evaluating applicants on the basis of digital portfolios has the potential to create a different K–12 universe. Instead of being pushed to produce numbers, students would be encouraged to create bold initiatives—a science experiment, a novel, or a fund-raiser for a classmate's family devastated by a drive-by shooting. Kids can take intellectual risks and learn to handle setbacks and failures. High school is less about ranking kids and more about helping them acquire competencies that empower them to make their world better. If successful, the Coalition could restore authenticity to high school and align "college ready" with "life ready."

Still fragile, the Coalition for Access has its detractors, particularly those excelling in today's college admissions game. During the year, I met several, with exchanges laid out in Table 3.1.

An admissions dean for a top-ranked university shared an added objection to relying on portfolios of authentic work. Many college courses, especially introductory courses, are taught in large lecture halls and require students to take accurate notes and memorize content. An entering freshman without this training might well hit the wall. So we need bad high school pedagogy to train kids for bad college pedagogy. At least he was honest.

TABLE 3.1 The Coalition for Access Application: Point / Counterpoint

Their Objection	My Rebuttal
Rich kids will game the system.	They're crushing it already.
Heaven forbid if ninth-graders start worrying about college.	Rich families obsess about college when their baby is in the womb. If poor kids wait until they're juniors, it's probably too late.
The new application is ambiguous.	So is life. Ambiguity rewards creativity, which is harder to delegate to a parent or consultant.
Reviewing digital portfolios is too much work for college admissions officers.	High school shouldn't be defined by what's convenient for college admissions officers.

Cleveland, Ohio—The saying "What gets measured gets done" permeates education. Schools teach to tests they're held accountable to. High schools judged by college placements embrace "college ready." Students valued for their AP scores will spend the school year preparing for AP exams. If we represent the accomplishments of four years in high school with a one-page transcript, students will organize their time to produce the best possible transcript.

Scott Looney, head of Cleveland's Hawken School, has a bold plan to change American education. He believes the current transcript is obsolete, impeding innovation and real learning. It's tied to seat time and grades, organized by isolated subjects. GPA calculations give extra credit for "advanced" classes, pushing kids to jam schedules with AP courses. Class-ranking competition turns high school into a kind of *Hunger Games*. Fearing any possibility of a bad grade, students avoid risky answers and dodge hard courses. Grades corrode intrinsic motivation and suffer from inconsistency and rampant inflation. Those tidy boxes for extracurriculars push kids to take on sound-bite experiences. Compelling criticisms.

Scott is working with other leading private schools to redesign the high school transcript. There's precedent for his strategy. In 1952, three private high schools (Lawrenceville, Andover, and Exeter) and three colleges (Harvard, Yale, and Princeton) collaborated to create what became the AP curriculum, awarding college credit for advanced work in high school. Ironically, many top private schools have dropped AP to offer students deeper learning experiences, although AP now pervades America's mainstream high schools.

Looney argues, what if applicants from top high schools submit twenty-first-century transcripts? If just one school took this approach, the headmaster would be shown the door. But if enough top schools band together around a next-generation transcript, there's safety in numbers. Pave the way for a modernized transcript, and then make it available broadly. Change the high school transcript, and you change high school. What gets measured gets done.

The Mastery Transcript replaces subjects with critical skills, grades with levels of mastery, and test scores with authentic portfolios of student work. This transcript is designed so that an admissions officer can review it in ten minutes or so. The approach resembles how schools of art and music evaluate candidate portfolios, or how the Boy and Girl Scouts use merit badges to capture accomplishment. This accountability model would enable those with oversight responsibility (e.g., boards, superintendents, legislators) to audit sample transcripts for a school or district, benchmark performance, and identify underperformers.

At 10 p.m. after a long day, the energetic Looney quoted Buckminster Fuller: "You never change things by fighting the existing reality. To change something, build a new model that makes the existing model obsolete." By the end of 2016, over one hundred schools had committed to supporting the www.mastery.org initiative.

A Cleveland community forum included Erin Frew, the principal of Cleveland's New Tech West high school, one of two hundred New Tech Network schools that live and breathe project-based learning. Frew's students take on challenges that "mimic what adults do as part of the world of work. They need to solve a problem. Information is gathered and analyzed to produce a solution. Students work together in teams to efficiently learn the material so that they can create an excellent solution." PEAK. The kids at Frew's school would be prime beneficiaries of Scott's mastery transcript. Well-crafted interdisciplinary projects don't map onto a traditional transcript but align with the mastery transcript. No more trade-offs between better learning and a better transcript.

Nothing would transform K–12 schools faster than a college admissions process that values creative, authentic student work. The efforts of Nondorf and Looney could be a major advance. If you're a college graduate, push your alma mater to join the Coalition for Access and welcome digital portfolios as a key part of an application. If you're involved in a high school, call their attention to the Mastery Transcript Consortium.

Assessment frameworks tied to digital portfolios and essential competencies proffer an added, less obvious, benefit. It's trendy to hold that STEM is *the* path to an exciting career, despite the successes of so many non-STEM people in all walks of life. Everything changes with a focus on essential skills. A student can demonstrate communications mastery through an English essay, or a lab report. Show their critical analysis skills through a philosophy critique, or a math proof. Exhibit technology skills through a project, not a set of courses or a major. Subject areas become a means to mastering underlying competencies that enable students to thrive in a world where machine intelligence is the ultimate subject matter expert.

It's important to distinguish between teaching someone a subject and helping them learn to think like an expert in the field. Should our kids study history facts, or learn to think like a historian? Memorize science definitions, or learn to think like a scientist? Answer canned questions about a poem, or learn to think like a literature critic? Drill on math microtasks, or learn to think like a creative mathematician? Every school claims to teach its students to think, but few do. When we push kids along a content-laden college-ready path, they're rewarded more for memorizing than thinking—a balance that would shift dramatically if students were assessed on the basis of authentic and creative work.

I need to make one last, critical point about "college ready." Our education system downplays the study of statistics, then draws on flawed statistical analyses to support the status quo. Shrewd. Numerous studies assert that a college degree is the best single investment a young adult can make, yielding a substantial lifetime earning differential. These analyses are problematic. There's adverse selection in the populations. They predict the future based on the past, like driving a car by looking in the rearview mirror. Multitudes of loan-burdened college dropouts muddy the statistical waters. But by far the biggest failing of these studies is that they ignore the consequences of an education system that prepares students for just one path: college. Students leave K–12 schools with no hirable competencies. If they forego college, their only alternative is a lousy minimum-wage job, and even those go increasingly to overqualified college graduates. We'd reach different conclusions about the lifetime value of an expensive college degree if high school graduates had hirable proficiencies—an outcome precluded by our self-perpetuating college-ready focus.

The Ivory Tower

We need a broad spectrum of words for "college." There are all sorts. Some provide outstanding experiences for almost all students; some are good options for certain students; some are expensive places where learning goes to die. Some colleges ensure affordability for every student; others are ruthlessly predatory. Some are intimate; some are factories. Some are committed to effective pedagogy; others just want to goose their *U.S. News & World Report* rankings. Some students make the most of the opportunity; other stumble through in a chemically mood-modified haze. There are the distinct phases of college: admissions, intro courses, more advanced courses, and graduate school. So when you use the word "college," caution is the watchword.

For adults who graduated from a respected residential university, college evokes fondness and nostalgia. It was your first real experience with independence, affording time to mature. You forged lifetime friendships amid fun and challenge. You were exposed to interesting ideas. You carry with you indelible memories of pranks, parties, sports events, and wacky adventures. Your alma mater is core to your identity—as evidenced by your clothes, your wedding party, and your last will and testament. This experience shaped you profoundly, and you believe every child deserves the same.

I often ask adults to describe the college experiences that had the biggest impact on them. To date, no one has responded, "My lecture courses." The groundbreaking research of Richard Arum and Josipa Roksa explains this in *Academically Adrift*. Over a six-year period, they tracked the learning of some 2,300 undergraduates at two dozen colleges and observed "no statistically significant gains in critical thinking, complex reasoning, and writing skills for at least 45% of the students in the study" after two years of college. Across all students, gains were minimal in four years of college, leading the authors to conclude, "An astounding proportion of students are progressing through higher education today without measureable gains in general skills as reported by the [Collegiate Learning Assessment]."[5] That so little is learned is due to a combination of poor college pedagogy and student work ethics straight from *Animal House*. These findings accord with surveys of employers, who report that college isn't preparing its students for professional life.

Without doubt, college transforms many young adults. For kids from challenging circumstances, it can offer special magic, widening their horizons as it lifts them out of poverty. But a discussion of college demands an unclouded view of changes in the college landscape, as shown in Table 4.1.

Given these shifts, colleges ought to be motivated to improve their value proposition. But changing a college is hard. Just walk in the shoes of a college president. Loyal and generous alumni

TABLE 4.1 The Changing College Landscape

	1977	2017
Cost of a Four-Year Degree		
Public	~ $4,000	~ $75,000
Private	~ $8,000	~ $225,000
College Course Availability	Only for Enrollees	Free & Online
Path to a Good Job	Excellent	Problematic

want their alma mater to be just as it was that autumn day they moved into their freshman dorm. Tenured faculty take pride in an Ivory Tower steeped in history and tradition. These inveterate academicians often view teaching as a distraction from research, see no reason to change, and can ignore anyone who thinks otherwise.

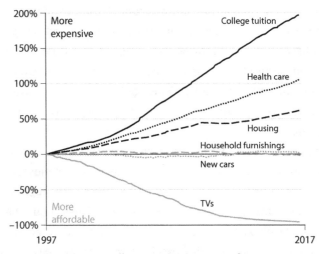

FIGURE 4.1. Skyrocketing College Costs. *Source:* Data from American Enterprise Institute.

Thankfully, there are sparks of innovation in higher education. Respect is growing for the work-study and project-intensive programs of schools like Northeastern University, Waterloo, Olin College, and Purdue. Stanford paints a vision of a different future (www.stanford.2025.com), where students pursue missions instead of majors as they cycle between on-campus study and real-world experience. And we're about to visit colleges that are innovating in how their students learn and how their institution helps level society's playing field.

Tempe, Arizona—Michael Crow, president of Arizona State University (ASU), is orchestrating the single most consequential overhaul of a major four-year university in our nation's history. Situated in Tempe, with satellite campuses across the state, ASU now educates some 100,000 students. Justifiably, it was recently named the nation's most innovative university. After serving as provost of Ivy League Columbia, Crow took over ASU's presidency in 2002. During his tenure, enrollment has almost doubled. Its student population is now every bit as diverse as Arizona's. Retention and completion rates have risen substantially. He's changed ASU from "a faculty-centered culture to a student-centered culture." He asks the hard question of "Why are we here?" He believes that the university's role is to "be transformative on a social scale," and he's making that happen.

Vital to Crow's success is his willingness to walk away from conventional measures of a university's quality. He notes that most schools take pride in an exclusivity based on rejecting most applicants—which he terms "a false status." His take? Colleges should be valued for developing excellence in the students they admit, not for admitting students with excellent test scores. ASU is about access, affordability, and student success. Crow gives his faculty high-level goals, but trusts them as lead designers of the new ASU. Some rise to this challenge, while others grouse, but on the whole it's working.

ASU is experimenting with online offerings but recognizes that online content is only a small part of the learning equation. These courses include lots of interpersonal interaction and support—face-to-face or online, among students, and between students and faculty. Course designers understand that people learn by engaging in debate and interaction with others, not by passively watching a lecture. This insight escaped the horde of universities who jumped on the MOOC (Massive Open Online Course) bandwagon a couple of years ago, with disappointing results. Somehow, watching a video lecture and pausing occasionally to answer multiple-choice quiz questions isn't all that transformational.

ASU is shifting its model from seat time to competency/mastery-based learning, enabling students to earn full course credit at a pace matching proficiency. They've launched a dozen interdisciplinary schools focused on society's biggest challenges: urban development, national security, sustainable energy. Research funding has grown substantially, and the school now generates tens of millions of dollars each year in technology transfer license fees. They're offering high school students opportunities to earn university credit.

ASU is thriving with a distinctive combination of academic excellence, applied learning, and diversity. They attract more National Merit Scholars than any other top state university, including UCLA and Berkeley. They produce more Fulbright scholars than many Ivy League colleges. Almost half of ASU students are Pell-eligible. First-generation college students comprise 40% of their student body. Crow's book *Designing the New American University* lays out his vision of inclusivity, affordability, and innovation. This vision isn't without controversy, labeled by some academics as "terrifying" or "dystopian." But some 150 colleges have visited to learn more about ASU's model.

Olympia, Washington—Experiential-learning pioneer Evergreen State College was founded in 1971 under legislation signed into law by the then-governor Dan Evans, one of his many impressive contributions during a long career of public service. Evans, who was also a two-term U.S. senator, is the kind of reasonable moderate who has disappeared from today's political landscape. From 1977 to 1983, he served as Evergreen's second president and has stayed involved since. Sharp as a tack at age ninety-one, Evans explains Evergreen's commitment to experiential learning:

> Most college students still go to institutions that teach in the style of the last century—individual courses, taught in

specific subject siloes, the compilation of which adds up to a major and graduation. But life isn't like that, separated and organized exquisitely. Life is complicated, sometimes messy, and almost never predictable. Here at Evergreen, coordinated study programs, student participation in helping to design their education, group and individual contracts, and a dedicated teaching faculty combine to prepare students well for that world ahead.

In Evergreen's early days, Evans as sitting governor got an irate call from a parent whose son had enrolled recently. The father asked his son, "What courses are you taking?" The son's terse response, "Sailing." The father follows, "That's nice. What else are you taking?" Back to the son, "Nothing." Angry to the point of sputtering, the father called Evans demanding, "What's going on at Evergreen?" Evans patiently explained that the son was part of a small group of students working closely with four faculty members. They were immersed in intensive seminar discussions on literature relating to the sea, the economics of ocean commerce, the math and physics of wind propelling a boat through the water, and the history of exploration by sea. They were learning five disciplines and their interrelationships, all in a real-world context.

To this day, Evergreen is committed to providing students with affordable, life-changing experiences. Tuition is just $6,300 for in-state residents, and they accept almost all applicants. They offer the ultimate in flexibility, both on and off campus. Students wanting to master a foreign language are encouraged to create their own learning experience abroad. Students with a passion for a given field are encouraged to seek out real-world learning experiences. The school looks for ways to accept credit for work done elsewhere—at another college or in the real world. Students stepping off the college track, whether for a few months or a few years, don't face bureaucratic hassles in returning. Their focus is student success, not revenue. Their long list of successful alumni includes Lynda Weinman, founder and CEO of the successful Lynda.com, who credits Evergreen as the place where she learned "to be in charge of her future."

─ ─ ─ ─ ─   ╲╲│╱╱   ─ ─ ─ ─ ─

Budgets reveal organizational values. Some admirable outliers invest in improved pedagogy and scholarships for low-income students. Others direct capital to plush student dorms, fancy campus centers, sports stadiums and training compounds, private jets, and initiatives to boost those pernicious *U.S. News & World Report* rankings. During the spring, campus lawns are dotted with FAFSA signs urging students to keep their financial aid forms current. Many students can't graduate in four years because of logjams with required, but overbooked, courses—upping their all-in cost of college. Some universities now charge more for

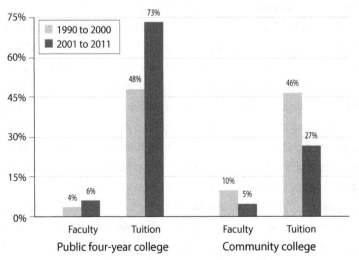

FIGURE 4.2. What Is Driving College Tuition Increases? *Source*: The College Board.

nicer dorms and food plans to generate incremental revenue, even though this policy effectively segregates affluent students from their low-income classmates.

Anchorage, Alaska—Herb Schroeder took a circuitous path to respected leadership of a top university engineering program. As a high school sophomore in Chicago, he flunked math. He was told to give up on STEM, and did . . . until age twenty-seven. After high school, he ventured north to Alaska for a construction job on the TransAlaska pipeline. Drawn into engineering, he enrolled at the University of Alaska, earned a BS in mechanical engineering and an MS and PhD in civil engineering. Along the way, he concluded that the way we teach STEM makes no sense. He gives students big design challenges—building bridges subject to design criteria, or designing a mechanism to lift an umbrella using parts from the local junkyard, or daring kids to make a functioning quad copter from basic RadioShack components. Engage them, challenge them, and let their STEM passion and expertise blossom. PEAK.

Over time, Schroeder became concerned, then alarmed, that few native Alaskans were pursuing STEM. Curious, he found that most natives enrolling in college were years behind in basic reading and math skills. Their high school STEM courses were mostly taught by non-natives skeptical that natives could handle challenging work. Many natives by age eighteen become convinced they have no future in STEM—just as Herb had. So he proposed starting the Alaska Native Science and Engineering Program (ANSEP), and skeptics "almost ran me out of the state." Now in its twenty-second year, ANSEP has produced some four hundred native Alaskan graduates with STEM degrees, with another two thousand in the sixth-grade through PhD pipeline. He's broadening its reach to non-STEM pursuits and to middle and high school natives. He's showing what Alaskan native kids are capable of and is creating the next generation of great scientists and engineers among the native population. Yet, Herb told me, "people are still arguing about whether our approach works. So many educators and parents are reluctant to step outside of the lines."

Baltimore, Maryland—Freeman Hrabowski, the president of the University of Maryland, Baltimore County (UMBC), is the real deal. He grew up in Birmingham, Alabama, the son of two teachers. His father left teaching to become a steelworker because "he could make more money doing that." At age twelve, Hrabowski was part of the Children's Crusade for Civil Rights. He was arrested, spent five days in jail, and was spat on by Birmingham's public safety commissioner, "Bull" Connor. Upon leaving jail, he was told by Martin Luther King Jr. that these actions would "have an impact on generations as yet unborn." Hrabowski's made good on MLK's prediction.

Hrabowski graduated with high honors in math from Hampton Institute, followed by a PhD from the University of Illinois with a dissertation combining statistics and higher education administration. When he joined UMBC as vice provost in 1987, it was a sleepy commuter school in a poor city rife with racial tension. Plenty of aspiring scientists were coming to UMBC but flunking out. Within five years, Hrabowski became president and embarked on wholesale redesign—emphasizing hands-on learning connected to the surrounding community. He didn't shy from controversy, shutting down Africana studies and their football team, directing resources to STEM and a chess team that went on to win championships. Not easy moves.

Hrabowski points to three issues that turn kids off from school, especially STEM. "School is boring. We teach kids to think mechanically. And we don't connect STEM to the real world." He went on. "People need to understand how mechanical we've been. Any person who took high school math is familiar with the term 'function.'

But if you ask, 'What the hell is a function?' they don't know. Even math teachers and engineers often struggle with something so basic." He cited a study that found that the biggest fallout in STEM at elite universities is among high-achieving students who, after years of academic success, stumble in a "weeder-outer" introductory course and seek refuge in a safer major.

At UMBC, I met four upperclassmen pursuing degrees in neuroscience, chemical engineering, and computer science, all on track to earn PhDs. These young adults, all of color from poor families, had full scholarships through UMBC's Meyerhoff Scholars program—a national model for fostering STEM scholarship in the African American community. At UMBC, projects "keep on coming." They've all done one or more internships with organizations that include the Army Research Lab, Lincoln Lab, Northrop Grumman, and Engineers Without Borders. One noted, "I had a tough time in circuits until I built a radio. Then I understood." He got hooked on STEM through robotics. One hated science in high school ("If you don't know the periodic table, you're not good at chemistry") but is now majoring in neuroscience, motivated by her best friend's schizophrenia. Another was planning on majoring in music, got interested in the global water crisis, and is now a chemical engineering major. The fourth talked about making her own beauty products—"Titration lab has a whole new meaning when you know its value." All said the same thing: "Until UMBC, I didn't think black people did science." These impressive kids are blazing a path forward, becoming impressive STEM leaders and inspiring other minority kids to pursue STEM careers.

UMBC has grown its enrollment over the past decade by 18%, while increasing STEM enrollment by a whopping 48%. Among U.S. colleges, just one in four who start out as STEM majors survive to graduate. There's almost no fallout at UMBC, and some 40% of UMBC's graduates earn STEM degrees. Far more UMBC undergraduates went on to earn a PhD or MD in a STEM field during the years

2011–15 than from any other college in America. UMBC's annual research budget has soared from $1 million to over $80 million, with priority on funding undergraduate research. Today, UMBC has partnerships with about a hundred local businesses, providing students with internships and postgrad employment. Coming full circle, businesses started by faculty or alums are now UMBC partners.

While running a college would seem all-encompassing, Hrabowski is changing Baltimore's K–12 inner-city schools. With a $1.6 million grant from Northrop Grumman, he's equipping schools with hands-on STEAM (science, technology, engineering, art, math) programs and training teachers in project-based learning. He's bringing education resources to adults in the community by establishing local STEAM centers—a science lab, makerspace, digital video and sound studio, parent resource room, and community meeting space. He's helping high school kids access internships. "Young scholars can do much more, much sooner than we expect. We're seeing companies give high school kids certification and security clearances. Apprenticeships and internships are key for high school kids, helping them connect what they learn to life."

Oh, in his spare time, Hrabowski works with the Department of Juvenile Services to help young first-time offenders. Hrabowski relates, "They have amazing skills if only we get them away from destructive to constructive. They are great thinkers, with great emotional intelligence. If I give them a word problem, they blow me away. But school is so boring, and they develop a self-view of being a bad person."

For all of these kids, Hrabowski says, "we are going to work to prepare these children to compete against anybody, anywhere in the world."

These university STEM programs are exciting, but I want to advocate for the liberal arts. Today, almost all college students cite future employment as their primary objective, leading them—

often with help from tuition-paying parents—to major in something practical. Well, I double-majored in English and physics, and attribute my success in technology businesses more to my English classes than my undergraduate physics work or my PhD in engineering. My literature courses helped me learn to communicate and to critically analyze. The issue with the liberal arts isn't the failure to prepare students for careers. It's the failure to convince adults—parents and employers—that liberal arts majors develop relevant competencies. Throughout my career, I avoided interviewing business majors, preferring candidates with the self-confidence to major in something unconventional and intellectually challenging. That worked out just fine and made for more interesting interviews. But I'd offer this advice to liberal arts faculty who view marketing as undeserving of Ivory Tower status: your field needs it.

Annapolis, Maryland—One of the world's most innovative education institutions is the U.S. Naval Academy (USNA). From stem to stern, Vice Admiral Ted Carter, the Academy's superintendent, and his team are innovating in how they prepare midshipmen for their careers.

Admiral Carter takes pride in how Navy pilots are creative and unpredictable, contrasting them with by-the-books Air Force pilots. At age twenty-seven, he was a Top Gun instructor. In 1999, he commanded an F14 squad on the *Theodore Roosevelt* aircraft carrier, flying raids over Kosovo with a team of fifteen inexperienced pilots. He decided to give every pilot equal flying time, not just concentrate on the better pilots. And he described what he called his greatest teaching experience:

> Every night at midnight, we'd all meet in the ready room. I called it learning by humility. We talked openly about things

we did poorly, mistakes we made. I led by talking about what I had done wrong, setting the tone. These sessions raised our collective learning exponentially, and our squad had a much higher success rate than others, with greater morale and trust. If we had had the mind-set of zero defects, of no mistakes, we'd never learn and we'd never innovate. As it was, we were fearless in figuring out new tactics, including a classified breakthrough in how to guide bombs in horrible weather.

Carter talked about changes he's made in USNA admissions policy. "We put a lot more value on life experiences. Has this candidate overcome adversity in her or his life? Before, we emphasized SATs, class rank, whether someone was an Eagle Scout. With our new priorities, we get a more diverse entering class. For our most recent entering class, less than 40% were white male. Some 28% were female. We're finding that by prioritizing candidates who have demonstrated the ability to overcome adversity, we not only get a more diverse group, but our graduation rates and class performance are going up." He went on about the tenacity and grit he's seeing in entering classes stemming, in part, from their new admissions criteria. Of last year's entering class of 1,178 middies, only nine dropped out after their rigorous orientation program. Not one entering woman dropped out.

Carter spoke with justifiable pride about Navy's 2015 football team, their best since 1963. The team went 11–2, was ranked nationally, and played in a major Bowl game. What was Admiral Carter most proud of? Amid all of the fanfare and on-field success during the hectic fall semester, each of the team's seventeen seniors had either their best or second best academic semester while at the Academy.

CDR Kevin Mullaney chairs the USNA's Department of Leadership, Ethics, and Law. With a BS in engineering, he started his career as a nuclear engineer but shifted gears to get his PhD in organizational psychology. At Annapolis since 2004, he's helping shape the Academy's education strategy. He explained how entering students often have the mind-set of "Tell me what I need to know so I can reproduce it on a test and get a good grade." Over the past decade, their courses have evolved to feature project-based learning, Socratic seminars, and capstone projects. PEAK. He taught a course that included a simulation on containing pandemic diseases. His students reviewed instructions in advance, but Mullaney related, "no one knew what to do until they dove in and started playing." The story of learning.

Each year, teams of middies create initiatives designed to improve Academy operations. They come up with ideas, research the issues, write a proposal, and analyze impact. In the process, students take ownership for their institution while learning important things—like the rationale for existing routine or the challenges in convincing others. Teams with the top proposals present to the commandant; many have been implemented, including the popular recommendation to extend weekday liberty.

The USNA is all about leadership. All first-year middies address fundamental character questions: What are your distinctive skills and traits? What shapes you from the outside? How will you become a leader of character? In their first year, each student writes an aspirational paper: "Who Do I Want to Be as a Senior?" Students leverage experiences across all activities—classes, brigade, clubs, athletics, and summer training. Every student aspires to a vision of what kind of leader they'll be, getting perspective from faculty who have dealt with leadership challenges like deciding who will live and die. Most feedback comes from peers, reducing demands on faculty. Imagine if high schools took this approach to helping students become leaders.

These colleges show us that a university with exceptional leadership can innovate. They're making learning real, and affordable. They're admitting students for character, potential, and drive. They're performing at a high level because of diversity, not despite it.

Each year, about four million young adults leave our K–12 school system, half from families in poverty. Almost all of our three thousand colleges face financial challenges. Collectively, our universities can't offer enough scholarships to make college the vehicle for broad and equitable opportunity across America. If we continue to insist on a college degree to get to life's starting line, affluent kids will be fine but only a smattering of low-income kids will make it through. Millions are at risk.

It's trendy for politicians to push for free college. More precisely, for free tuition, for low- and middle-income students, for state colleges. While it might appear that the cavalry is coming to the rescue, these proposals are problematic. Their adverse impact on already tight college budgets will lead to more batch processing of students, at the expense of real learning. Our poorest families aren't likely to benefit, since they can't afford the considerable costs beyond tuition. "Free college" reinforces the current obsolete model, while shifting costs from certain families to the general taxpayer. Another piece of fool's gold that distracts us from the challenge of reimagining education.

Any college committed to educating kids from challenging circumstances is making an unequivocally positive contribution to our society. But our best path to leveling society's playing field is to make the high school diploma meaningful. Let students take on real-world challenges, gaining the ability to contribute effectively to an organization or a community. Ensure K–12 graduates have hirable skills. Encourage K–12 districts to offer dual credit opportunities to high school kids, letting them jump-start careers and get a cost-effective leg up on college. Push colleges to improve their value proposition by awarding credit for demonstrated competency and real-world experience. Turn the world upside down. Push higher education to better meet the needs of our students instead of pushing our students to better meet the needs of higher education.

\\|//

Augusta, Maine—Bill Beardsley, Maine's acting commissioner of education, served for twenty-two years as president of Husson University. No newcomer to education, Beardsley worries about our country's "college at any cost" mentality, especially since many demanding jobs don't require a college degree. He points to Maine's Jackson Lab, home of Nobel Laureates, where 75% of the employees never went to college. He's pushing proficiency models for graduation, with more options leading directly to fulfilling careers. He told a joke about a neurosurgeon dealing with back-to-back surgeries in the operating room but having to rush home to meet a plumber. The plumber comes, fixes the broken pipe in fifteen minutes, and hands her a $250 invoice. The surgeon complains, "Hey, that's more than I make in an hour." The plumber responds, "I know. I used to be a surgeon."

Driving around New England, I saw college after college I'd never heard of—Dean College, Atlantic Union College, Marlboro College, Becker College, Hellenic American University, and Beardsley's Husson University. These anonymous colleges are everywhere. Some provide students with solid educations, affordable tuition levels, acceptable graduation rates, and decent job prospects, but many don't. As marginal colleges scramble to fill spots, they blanket high school seniors with acceptance letters. Students react with "OMG! I've been accepted to college," trusting that doors have just opened to a better life. They often get seductive scholarships presented as, "We are so impressed with your accomplishments that we're offering you our esteemed $12,500 annual presidential scholarship. Over your time at our outstanding college, we'll be investing a total of $50,000 in your future success!" Thrilled to realize the dream we've convinced them to have, they commit to attend and sign papers locking them into substantial loans. Some graduate, only to find that a degree from an anonymous college doesn't take you all that far. Others drop out with a debt load they'll carry for the rest of their minimum-wage-earning life. We owe our kids—whether from privilege or fighting their way out of poverty—a K–12 education that equips them with the competencies—especially critical analysis and financial literacy—needed to steer clear of these education potholes.

Tallahassee, Florida—R. Jai Gillum heads the financial literacy initiative for the United Way in Tallahassee. Her programs help adults and school kids advance their understanding of financial issues, working with offerings from EverFi and Reality Store. She notes how few adults, irrespective of how they did in school, have a grasp of personal finance. There seems to be no limit to the ways a young adult can fall into a deep financial bind due to naïveté. One issue surprised me. A responsible young adult applies for credit for the first time, only to learn that she's deep in debt through no fault of her own. Gillum described cases where financially strapped adults take out credit cards in the name of a young child in their care and rack up thousands of dollars of debt. Too often, this adult isn't even part of the child's life when the scam comes to light.

After talking about her students, R. Jai told me about her own experience at Florida A&M University, where credit card companies dot the campus. She got several, confident she understood their financing terms. She set a limit of $500 on one card's balance, yet ended up with $3,000 of debt on it. When she fell behind on her payments, her interest rate ballooned to 27%. It took her ten long years to finally pay off this debt, a lesson shaping her career choice. Gillum pointed to Alex Sink, who ran unsuccessfully for governor of Florida. Sink called for incorporating financial literacy into high school curriculum, influenced by her own daughter's experience at Wake Forest. The daughter's overdrawn bank account triggered large monthly payments at stratospheric interest rates. Sink, an investment banker by background, saw firsthand the urgency in ensuring that our high school students are financially literate. If her own daughter, growing up in a banking-savvy home, made decisions that pulled her into a financial quagmire, how many other college-age kids are making naïve decisions locking in financial hardship?

Austin, Texas—Ben Bhatti, education advisor to Governor Greg Abbott, helps shape his state's public schools. He comes to public policy after teaching third-graders in Atlanta and then earning a law degree. He advises Abbott on the Texas DOE's budget and operational effectiveness, along with legislative priorities such as a recent bill to allow "eighth-grade students to pick different high school pathways more tailored to a skill set, leaving them better prepared for college or the workforce." He added, "We got rid of the Algebra II requirement, giving freedom to students to take other courses to get into community colleges." Ben is passionate about partnerships connecting public schools to local organizations to make classroom learning real. He shared this powerful anecdote:

> There's a student in Austin, a quiet girl, who came up to me and said, "Before I worked in project-based learning I would never have given a presentation or talked in front of everyone. Now I can." Seeing that get unlocked in her was critical for me. And she unlocked it in herself, the teacher was just facilitating. That next generation is so different from previous generations. Their ability to access information gives them a different way of looking at the world. If we don't facilitate that, it's going to be a big lost opportunity. The current system

isn't moving students to explore that. Testing is dumbing down their ability to explore and learn. Facilitating real learning is critical. Education is no longer sitting in a classroom and telling them what's going on; they have to relate what they're learning in a classroom out to their life.

Bhatti produced the documentary *eduCAUTION*, which every high school student, parent, guidance counselor, and education policymaker should see. It's that good. The film takes dead aim at the student loan crisis, college, and the American Dream. It offers sobering data along with powerful interviews of students struggling with loans up to $400,000. While it includes famous politicians (Barack Obama, Marco Rubio, Elizabeth Warren), I was blown away by Representative Karen Bass (D-CA), whose daughter was killed in a car crash. Almost immediately, Bass starting getting letters and calls from creditors demanding full repayment of the daughter's outstanding student loans. When they requested a copy of the death certificate, Bass provided it, only to find that the creditors then transferred the loan obligation, taken on by her adult daughter, to Bass. With a heavy heart, Bass adds,

> To this day, and she's been gone for six years, I get letters and phone calls for her, demanding payment, even though I have told them repeatedly that she's no longer here.

A few decades ago, college more or less guaranteed an attractive entry-level job. We still behave as though that's true, but that guaranteed good job is now a crapshoot. Of young Americans who begin at a four-year college, about half graduate in a reasonable time frame. Of those, about half get a good job. Meanwhile, college costs have increased by 8% *annually* for the past three decades. To cope with skyrocketing costs, we've opened the

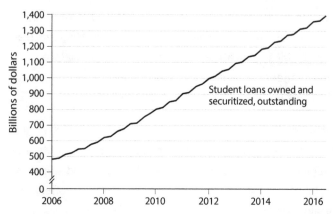

FIGURE 4.3. Massive Student Loan Debt. *Source:* Data from Federal Reserve Economic Data.

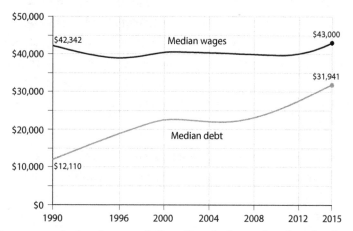

FIGURE 4.4. Student Loans and Wage Growth. *Source:* Based on data from Brad Hershbein, W. E. Upjohn Institute for Employment Research; U. S. Department of Education; Federal Reserve Bank of New York; Mark Kantrowitz as published in the *Huffington Post* (Shahien Nasiripour and Nicky Forster, "3 Charts That Show Just How Dire The Student Debt Crisis Has Become," March 22, 2017).

student-loan spigots. Some 71% of 2015 college grads left with an average student loan debt of $35,000. A total of 43 million U.S. adults carry outstanding student loans that average $30,000, and some 25% are in default. Somewhat incredibly, 2.8 million adults age sixty or older are still paying off their student loans. Student loan debt can dog someone for a lifetime, since it's the one form of debt that can't be shaken through personal bankruptcy. Congress, in its wisdom, made it easy to get student loans and almost impossible to default on them.

The financial overhang of college leads many young adults to steer clear of satisfying careers that offer modest salaries or doing anything as risky as starting their own business. Conditioned to jump through hoops and financially pressured, they trod to the career services office, apply for interviews, and take the highest-paying offer. A Faustian bargain. An American College Health Association's survey underscores a different form of damage. Of college students surveyed in 2015, 85.6% felt "overwhelmed," 47.7% reported feeling that "things were hopeless," 34.5% reported "feeling so depressed that it was difficult to function," and 8.9% seriously considered suicide.[6]

------   \|/   ------

New York, New York—New York City is a hotbed of start-ups disrupting traditional higher education. They view mainstream universities as giant ocean liners steaming full speed ahead toward an iceberg field, bickering over the dinner menu. These smart, aggressive teams are offering compelling options that transform a student's career prospects, cost- and time-effectively. They are getting traction.

NYC's General Assembly offers twelve-week immersive courses in coding, web design, data analytics, graphic design, marketing, and general business. GalvanizeU's NYC center offers affordable twenty-four-week immersives in website design and data sciences, connecting students to industry experts, innovative businesses, and rising start-ups. Start-up Revature is partnering with the City University of New York to offer its graduates a free twelve-week immersive camp where they acquire technology-related skills enabling them to . . . actually get a job. The Flatiron School helps young adults turbocharge careers through a three-month immersion in coding, collaboration, and communication. Since inception, more than 98% of Flatiron's graduates have gotten one or more job offers, with an average starting salary of $74,000. They now accept just 6% of applicants.

These schools are showing that someone can elevate their life prospects without heading down a long and winding college road. In a matter of months, students gain certificates reflecting mastery. Some graduates will apply their new expertise for decades, some will move to other roles, and some will do something totally different after a couple of years. No matter, they leave these immersive programs in great shape, opening career doors without prohibitive debt.

Our country's community colleges are a powerful potential resource. Currently, they're viewed as a consolation prize for kids who can't make it to four-year college. Many are traditional in structure—subjects, lectures, two years of seat time to get an associate's degree, and "weeder-outer" prerequisites. Completion rates are abysmal. But these community colleges could reinvent themselves. Call themselves Career and Learning Accelerators. Award digital certificates for shorter-term immersive programs tied to career-elevating skills (e.g., graphic design, compelling writing, welding, computer programming), capabilities (e.g., sales, marketing, leadership, project management), or intellectual pursuits (e.g., Victorian literature, humanity's great philosophers). Train faculty in state-of-the-art pedagogy. Align courses with real-world challenges, internships, and mentors. Students return multiple times as their careers progress. Turn our nation's 1,500 community colleges into a strategic asset to help citizens at all stages in life—from high school to older workers in dead-end jobs—to turbocharge their skill sets and expand their minds.

Will our community colleges seize the day? Perhaps. In any case, a bevy of aggressive start-ups see higher education as a large market ripe for disruption. Don't underestimate what they'll accomplish.

Boston, Massachusetts—Eric Mazur chairs the Applied Physics Department of Harvard, having taught there for over thirty years with numerous teaching awards. He holds many patents and has started technology companies. Today, he is one of the world's most innovative educators, but it wasn't always this way. Mazur learned conventionally while in school and replicated this approach to the classroom in his first decade teaching at Harvard. He had every indication it was working, since he got rave reviews for his courses and his students excelled on exams.

About fifteen years ago, Eric came across a simple twenty-five-question test, designed to assess whether students understand the physical world. The Force Concept Inventory (FCI) Test, designed by professors at Arizona State University (ASU), includes simple questions like tracing the trajectory of a heavy object dropped from an airplane in flight. The ASU professors were reporting disturbing results—even their best physics students performed poorly. Eric's students had excelled in high school math and science (5s on AP Physics and Calculus BC, perfect SAT or ACT math scores, straight As), so he was confident they'd ace the FCI test. Well, their scores weren't much better than guesswork. He repeated the exam at the end of his course, expecting real improvement from academic achievers in a top-ranked course at esteemed Harvard. Only tiny gains, on the exact same exam.

Concluding that his students weren't learning real science, Mazur completely revamped his course. It now features Socratic debate on thought-provoking questions about how the world works, along with project-based learning that mirrors CTE. His students gain real insight into the physical world, which in turn makes the definitions and formulas meaningful . . . and memorable. He occasionally has his students take the final exam from a more conventional formula-driven physics course at Harvard, and they excel. When students from a traditional course take Eric's final, they fail. Mazur related to me a comment from a student's end-of-year review of his class: "I learned so much in this class. My only complaint is that Professor Mazur didn't teach us anything. We had to learn it all ourselves."

While in Massachusetts, I saw Eric in action. He posed the question in Figure 4.5 to a large group of educators. Clusters formed to debate what happens to the water level. With sky-high energy in the room, the "students" were driving the discussion, with Eric observing.

For five years, Mazur was a member of the AP Physics Advisory Committee. He pushed them to include questions like these on the AP Physics exam. To its credit, the College Board did field tests but ultimately rejected questions of this nature. The reason? Students who excelled at plugging numbers into formulas didn't do as well on questions about how the world worked, and vice versa.

A boat carrying a large boulder is floating on a small pond. The boulder is thrown overboard and sinks to the bottom of the pond.

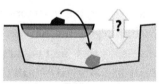

After the boulder sinks to the bottom of the pond, the level of the water in the pond is
1. higher than,
2. the same as,
3. lower than it was when the boulder was in the boat.

FIGURE 4.5. An Example of Eric Mazur's Physics Pedagogy. *Source*: Professor Eric Mazur, Harvard University.

With the overarching goal of producing a bell curve of results, these questions distorted the desired distribution and were discarded.

Just two miles down the Charles River sits the Massachusetts Institute of Technology (MIT), the world's most prestigious engineering institution. Surely MIT students are learning boatloads of science and engineering. Yet at a recent MIT commencement, a professor presented several graduates with a wire, a battery, and a lightbulb, challenging them to light up the bulb. None could produce a functioning circuit. On paper, they're extraordinary STEM students—the world's very best with stellar scores on every test you can think of. Yet they flail at something an electrician can do in a flash. Have these MIT graduates learned real science?

Several of Boston's top software developers and entrepreneurs met with me to talk about education. Many reported being lousy students but thrived in the creative world of software. They related that their organizations used to hire entry-level programmers through college recruiting. Now they rely heavily on GitHub, an open-source repository letting them directly evaluate a candidate's code—a digital portfolio of software. They're hiring high school dropouts, as well as grads of short-term immersive coding programs where "students learn more in three months than computer science majors learn in four years." Of four-year colleges, they prefer places like Olin, Northeastern, and Worcester Polytechnic Institute that feature project-based learning and internships. One noted about MIT and Harvard grads: "They don't learn much there that's relevant but think they have. Usually, their first three questions are about their title, salary, and how nice their office will be."

In one sense, these lessons might be narrow—maybe just that memorizing Coulomb's Law doesn't necessarily lead to understanding electricity. But suppose there's more. Suppose even our best students aren't learning much, something we saw signs of at

Lawrenceville Academy, at Harvard, at MIT. That being facile with academic formalism doesn't reflect deep learning or real-world insight. That competence can be demonstrated in many ways, few of which are valued in school. That education grounded in real-world understanding would help students across a wide spectrum of life paths, from the trades to the Ivory Tower.

Could it be right there in front of us? Our schools could be places with trusted teachers, engaged students, and PEAK learning. They could prepare our children for careers and citizenship, with meaningful learning that opens doors. We could realize upsides far beyond the modest increases in test scores we've sought, and failed to realize, for years. Profound upside, shared broadly across America. Upside in our grasp, if we can find the courage to walk away from those eight miserable words: "We have to be able to measure it."

Letting Go

America's school communities include some 80 million parents. About 40 million are far too involved in their child's education. About 40 million are far too removed. A few dozen have it pretty much right. Families face hard choices. Do you push your child hard along the conventional path? Or are you open to their creating a different route forward? It's a rare parent who will explain the trade-offs and support decisions that don't produce a résumé admired by relatives, friends, and college admissions. Not an easy choice, and one parents struggle with.

This year, I met many parents who seemed to sense they weren't helping their child but perhaps hoped I might assuage their guilt. They'd say, "We've done well in our courses, with a 4.35 GPA. We took five AP courses last year and will complete twelve by graduation. Last summer, we focused on SAT test prep, and our most recent scores were 745/780. Now we're working on our college essays." Or some variant, but always "We." And then that question hinting at misgivings: "That's what we have to do. Right?"

Parents often say, "You know, all I really want is for my child to be happy." It's what we want but so easy to lose sight of. Parents should read Mac Bledsoe's *Parenting with Dignity*. He argues that parents need to effect an orderly transfer of decision-making responsibility, from making 100% of your newborn's decisions to making 0% of your eighteen-year-old's decisions. Not just unimportant decisions. All decisions. Prepare your child to enter adulthood with the skills, experience, and confidence to make sound decisions. Bledsoe's advice is equally important to educators. Schools could view their role as producing self-motivated students who can learn on their own. But schools, like parents, get trapped in wanting to remain indispensable to their children.

_ _ _ _ _ \\|// _ _ _ _ _

Dover, Delaware—When a parent approached me at a forum in Delaware, I braced myself for hearing about her children. She started, though, with a perceptive point about the Committee of Ten's uncomplicated world. In today's world, we have to balance trade-offs—what colleges want, what twenty-first-century organizations want, and what leads to a fulfilling life. They're not the same. I kept waiting for her to bring up something about her child but after our short conversation, she thanked me and stepped aside. I wrote in my blog post, "She was so smart, and I'm kicking myself that I didn't get her name." I thought I'd heard the last of her.

Delaware native Brian Sowards started USEED, a company providing colleges with a platform connecting students pursuing a project with alums interested in funding it. Presently, thirty-five colleges work with USEED, supporting four thousand students. Here's USEED in action: A team of University of Washington (UW) students wanted to design, build, test, and race human-powered submarines for the demanding International Marine Advanced Technology Education competition on Arctic exploration. This complex design poses challenges around an underwater breathing apparatus conveyed by an efficient submersible. Students dive into powerful interdisciplinary learning tied to all PEAK principles. UW partnered with USEED to engage alumni support for the project and exceeded fund-raising goals. Funders received periodic updates full of suspense and achievement, a refreshing contrast to a form letter thanking them for donating to the annual fund.

Sowards, age thirty-six, grew up pursuing the violin, philosophy, earth science, and coding. At age sixteen, he started in the honors program at the University of Delaware but dropped out to launch a start-up. Before founding USEED in 2011, he had started a dozen other companies, five while in high school. Many failed, but this entrepreneur views them as "lessons," not indications he should find a safe job at DuPont. Late in our conversation Brian casually mentioned, "Oh, the woman you blogged about in Delaware. That's my mother." Taken aback, I set up my first mother–son interview to better understand this entrepreneur.

Katherine Von Duyke isn't your normal parent. She devours education books, citing Dewey, Montessori, and Holt as important influences. She didn't hesitate to homeschool young Brian—"I always valued what Brian had to say. It's been a constant discovery. It's remarkable to me who each young child can become as an adult." They bought a curriculum package but "just got tired and sent it back. The tiredness comes from a loss of a sense of agency. We started to ask, 'How do we construct the right learning environment?' " She believes that pushing a kid through rote curriculum robs them of their say in what they want to explore, which ultimately leads to boredom and fatigue. Back then, homeschooling was illegal in Delaware. "We were terrified of having our kids taken away by social services. It was a horrible threat to live under." Homeschoolers in her community banded together to form an adequately religious co-op to provide legal cover.

Things went smoothly until thirteen-year-old Brian informed his mom that he was ready to set his own agenda. She commented, "I was teaching him to think for himself, to self-direct, but it came at me a lot sooner than I was expecting." Even this progressive parent found it hard to let go. "How do you know they're learning? Where is the evidence of growth?" Brian noted, "All I cared about was having freedom to do what I wanted to do. I went through a back-and-forth where I would pick subjects, and study some based on falling in love with them, and others where I was just checking a box." He finished his high school requirements by age fifteen, although he still doesn't have an official diploma.

Their next crisis occurred when Brian dropped out of college, another hard pill for his mother to swallow. But she trusted him. As he set out in a direction completely decoupled from academics, she was getting her PhD in education. She noted the irony that "the day I defended my PhD thesis was the day my son, a high school and college dropout, was on the cover of the *Chronicle of Higher Education*." Brian commented, "What makes my mother unusual in our culture is that she doesn't equate being unsure with certain doom. A lot of parents believe if they aren't sure things are working out for their kids, then they have to step in and rescue them. We rob them of the discovery of who this little being will become. Yes, my mom worried about college, but I also felt her curiosity wanting to see what would happen."

In creating USEED, Brian "began to have this vision that there are many people like me who want to create, who enjoy learning together. But it can be hard to take on the system and carve out your own path. I thought how amazing it could be to empower others to create things. We are in the early days of learning to build community through digital, with a depth of purpose and intimacy." He stresses that the normal academic ritual skips over questions like, "Why are you doing this? Why is it important to you? To others?" So he formed a company putting these questions front and center.

If he had pursued something conventional, Brian believes he would have done what it took to excel. He noted, though, "everyone wants to create. The difference is whether you're willing to take on the system." As a recent parent, Brian is walking in his mother's shoes: "We think our job as parents is to provide security to our children, to tell them what markers to hit and when to hit them. We have an educational construct that says you will learn these things and then you will become a person with agency. But you never get there. The carrot keeps moving."

Over the course of my trip, I heard many stories about over-involved parents. Some may surprise you. Parents try to convince teachers to give their child a better grade, from high school down through the early grades. Parents choose their child's extracurriculars and sports. Parents handle the college admissions process. Once their child is off at college, parents text with frequent reminders, review and edit assignments, and contact professors (or even college presidents) to contest unsatisfactory grades. Parents request to join their college student for a job interview. Parents of a rejected applicant call an employer, arguing that their child really is self-directed. The low point? A parent called an employer to explain that their child couldn't make the scheduled interview but asked to fill in on the child's behalf. True stories heard this year from employers, faculty, and college presidents.

In some trip trivia, Dover was one of forty-two state capitals, and capitols, I visited this year. During my trip, state capitals took on unexpected significance with parents. A surprising number told me, "I realized something was wrong when my child had to memorize all fifty state capitals." Apparently this assignment strikes a nerve. It's something parents endured in school and now realize is pointless. I encourage them to imagine a modified assignment. Students research why the heck a state capital is where it is. Debate the merits of locating Delaware's capital in Dover versus Wilmington. Weigh in on California's 1849 decision to move its capital from Monterey to Sacramento. Replace rote memorization with a thought-provoking analysis of the reasons behind a capital's location. Teachers, students, and parents can make these small changes to transform mindless assignments into something compelling. As an added bonus, I found it became easy to remember each capital after thinking about its story.

Wallingford, Connecticut—During this school year, I generally avoided elite schools. I care most about mainstream America. While in Connecticut, though, I visited Choate Rosemary Hall, a private boarding school with a $400 million endowment, a 6:1 student-to-teacher ratio, an average class size of 12, and a spectacular campus that includes their new I.D. Lab for exploration and innovation. This isn't your normal high school.

Joining me at Choate was education thought-leader Dick Hersch, author of the brilliantly titled *Losing Our Minds*. During a community forum, a parent expressed a concern frequently voiced, particularly by the affluent. "My child is under too much stress." Left unsaid was that a major source of stress for the child is the parent obsessing about their child's performance. Hersch noted, "There are two kinds of stress. There's lousy external stress to excel on things the kid doesn't believe in. But there's healthy stress that comes from setting a big goal, and pushing yourself to excel in the face of challenges and deadlines." It's rare for someone to produce something they're proud of without feeling stress. The key is aligning student work with a sense of purpose.

Time at Choate underscored the vast differences in budget dollars for educating America's kids. The annual budget at private schools like Choate is about $60,000 per student-year. Well-off public schools in Connecticut operate on budgets of up to $30,000 per student year, while schools in the state's poor communities struggle to get by with budgets well below $15,000 per student-year. Sure, an occasional East Hartford kid gets a Choate scholarship, but for the most part our education system locks in cycles of privilege and poverty. Schools like Choate can play an important role in breaking the cycle—through scholarships and, perhaps more importantly, through leadership in reimagining school.

Social Equity

In our land of opportunity, we cherish the principle that every American has a fair chance in life. When it comes to children, this principle has special meaning. Back in history class, we studied the *Brown v. Board of Education* Supreme Court ruling calling for education in America to be "available to all on equal terms." Yet most people know we're falling short, that all children aren't getting a fair shake in our schools.

To right this wrong, our education policies have set their sights on the overarching goal of closing what they've termed the "achievement gap." They present charts and graphs showing differing performance levels for children grouped by ethnicity or family income. Performance, though, isn't based on authentic achievement but on differences in standardized test scores. The data we have are the data we use.

Go online and take a few standardized-test practice questions. Then ask yourself, "Absent an external push, would a child want to drill on these?" Few would. But parents—especially the affluent and well educated—understand the importance of these tests. They push their kids hard, starting early. Money is no object in purchasing the best resources—books, devices, apps. They enlist tutors, nannies, and Ivy League babysitters as reinforcements to give their child an edge. When their child's motivation flags, they step in with rewards ranging from a few bucks to a BMW. These kids are headed for the right side of the achievement gap.

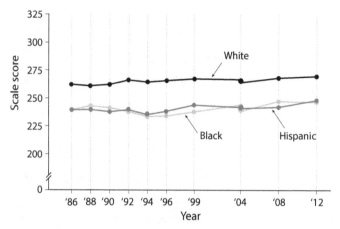

FIGURE 6.1. The Achievement Gap. *Source*: Data from National Center for Education Statistics.

Most children in challenging circumstances don't get this daily push. Children with only one overworked parent in their life aren't drilling at night on vocabulary flash cards or Motion Math. A teenager working long hours to help keep the family farm afloat doesn't have time for a Kumon tutor or SAT sleepover camp. They're building life skills through their daily challenges, but they aren't pushed to ace standardized tests. And when scores fall short, our solution is to pile on even more worksheets and test prep. Yet try as we might, this achievement gap stubbornly refuses to budge.

If our goal is to close a gap measured by standardized tests, we should give up. These tests reflect the parent's motivation, not the child's. Consider a more meaningful achievement gap: how students perform on messy real-world problems that require resourcefulness, out-of-the-box thinking, doggedness, and staring down failure. Authentic challenges get at a child's competencies, character, and intrinsic motivation—more than the parent's commitment. Over and over, educators relate to me their delight in seeing "underachieving" kids spring into accomplishment when taking on something they believe is important that aligns with their sense of purpose. This raises a profound question. If we aligned school with life, could we elevate learning for all kids, while closing an authentic achievement gap?

\|/

Jackson, Mississippi—With free time in Mississippi's capital, I typed "high school" into Google Maps, which led me to Lanier High School in downtown Jackson. What the heck? Just go to the front door and try to meet someone. Well, an administrator kindly gave me an impromptu tour, which provided a sobering look at social inequity in our schools.

Lanier High has a rich history, producing many alumni who were leaders of the civil rights movement and helping to desegregate Mississippi's schools. Today, though, Lanier's building and surrounding grounds are in shambles. A fenced-in area in the parking lot has a sign saying "Tennis Courts," but there are no nets. Its "walking path" is a tiny oval of crumbling concrete slabs surrounded by dirt, weeds, and broken glass. The school's interior is worse. Paint peeling, decrepit lockers, substandard lighting, and a smattering of out-of-date technology. I've visited many third-world schools; few are in worse shape than Lanier. My host estimated that her school's annual budget is well below $10,000 per student. She said recruiting teachers was difficult, and the good ones often leave when they find another opportunity. Many entering freshmen are years behind in reading skills. The student school day revolves around worksheets because "that's what we have to do." Some 40% drop out, and it's heroic that the faculty keeps it from being higher. I can't be certain of the school's ethnic composition, but everyone I saw there was African American.

Next stop Ridgeland High, just ten miles north of Lanier but it might as well be on a different planet. The outside grounds feature a large football stadium, along with two full-size practice football fields, all with lush turf. Their baseball stadium rivals most college facilities. A dozen adults were maintaining the grounds, with the smell of fresh-cut grass in the air. The building itself was impeccable, with state-of-the-art classrooms and labs.

Lanier sits in the midst of rundown housing and boarded-up stores. Ridgeland is surrounded by nice homes and malls with Brooks Brothers, Apple, J. Crew, and the Vintage Wine Market. Vast disparities in the local tax base translate into far more funding for Ridgeland. Across America, these differences often break strictly along racial lines. That wasn't the case here; the majority of Ridgeland's student body is minority. But whether discrimination is driven by income or race is of little consolation to Lanier High kids trying to claw their way forward in life.

Roseville, Minnesota—Brenda Cassellius, Minnesota's commissioner of education, has been a fighter all her life. She grew up in poverty and was homeless for some of her childhood. She credits Head Start for playing a decisive role in her life when she was young. In grade school, she helped her mom pay family bills by selling flowers on the streets of Minneapolis. A 1977 photo of nine-year-old Cassellius on a street corner with a bucket of flowers is both heartwarming and heartbreaking. She comes from a line of educators, including a grandfather who in the 1930s was president of the Black Teachers' Union in Norfolk, Virginia. Representing a group whose members were vastly underpaid relative to their white counterparts, he sued for equal pay and prevailed, with the help of a young lawyer named Thurgood Marshall. Again and again, her family told her she could be whatever she wanted in life. I suspect that even in their wildest dreams, they never imagined she'd be Minnesota's commissioner of education at age forty-three.

Cassellius works tirelessly to advance education for all of her state's children. She describes kids not graduating from high school because they missed a few questions on the required state math test—"On things they'll never use." She called the eleventh-grade math exam the great "weeder-outer" and fought successfully to relax these requirements. She pushed to establish "innovative districts" free of many bureaucratic requirements, but was disappointed that just three districts applied. She offered this metaphor: "If you chain up an elephant for prolonged periods, a funny thing happens when you remove the chains. It still thinks it can't go anywhere and stays in place for weeks. We've done the same thing to our educators. We've put them in standardized testing chains for decades. Now we need to remove the chains and make sure they know they're free to move forward." She spoke about young kids in poverty who hear a drumbeat of feedback about how they aren't proficient, instead of hearing the message of possibility she got from her family. "We can't keep doing this to our kids."

Bethel and Tuntutuliak, Alaska—Alaska has eight hub villages, each feeding a cluster of tribal villages. The only way you can get to them is by flying on one of Alaska's ubiquitous small prop planes that hop from one bumpy gravel airstrip to another. They're serious about weight limits and balancing on these planes. Bethel, one of the state's hub villages, has a total population of about four thousand. Several residents described being drawn to its raw beauty, but I wasn't seeing it. Its one loop road ties together a patchwork of stores, warehouses of corrugated metal, a few bad restaurants, one hotel fully meriting its one-star status, and living units that range from mobile homes to low-cost tract housing. There's so much trash on the ground that it's hard to tell where the dumpster stops and open spaces begin.

The NAEP scores of Alaska native kids in these remote villages are dismal. Many live in circumstances marked by alcoholism, drugs, physical and sexual abuse, and high suicide rates. In Bethel, a former senior administrator who spent a decade at the regional high school struggled with my questions. He wasn't sure about the graduation rates, texted someone, and then reported, "Around 50%." When asked why so low, "That's a good question. I'm not sure." When asked about graduation requirements, he indicated, "The usual. Language arts, two years of science, high school math, two years of a foreign language." The foreign language options? "German. Just German." Why? "That's the language taught by our foreign language teacher." Hmmm . . . I wonder why kids drop out.

There were bright spots in Bethel schools. An elementary school offers an early immersion language program, helping young children become proficient in Yupik, their ancestral language. Native elders are worried sick that their tribal language will disappear, since so many kids are now raised in homes dominated by satellite television and English-speaking adults. Waiting in Bethel's tiny airport for my flight to Tuntutuliak, I saw five happy teenagers. One was beating a tribal drum, and the others were dancing joyfully. When they paused, I introduced myself and asked about their school. They go to an alternative school in Bethel, explaining, "Our school is doing a great job of giving us the tools and skills we need to avoid getting trapped by drugs and alcohol." When I asked where they planned to live after graduating, they were uniform: "We want to stay here. This is our land. This is where our family is. Why would we want to leave?"

A quick flight over deserted tundra brought me to tiny Tuntutuliak, population 450. No roads. Just boardwalks and ATVs. Housing even more rudimentary than Bethel's, with many units lacking running water or indoor plumbing. Two small cluttered stores with overpriced items. Trash everywhere. A K–12 school, with fifteen dedicated teachers and about 150 kids. All part of a community that was fundamentally changed by the Hootch case, decided in 1972 by the Alaska Supreme Court. The ruling required Alaska to provide formal high school education to all Alaskan residents, no matter how remote the village. Bringing high school to a tribal village meant putting in place infrastructure to support imported non-native educators—transportation, stores, new buildings, and communications. This in turn brought exposure to satellite television, drugs, and alcohol. Once the genie was out, there's no putting it back for these subsistence villages.

Of the teachers at Tunt's school, about half were transplants, including a married couple there for over a decade. They live in small units, most with indoor toilet plumbing but lacking showers. Their "social life" is limited to the village's 450 people or expensive flights elsewhere. Even a short flight to Bethel for a weekend costs $260. So teachers spend most of the school year in the village. They have Internet access and make lots of purchases through Amazon, which supports free shipping for Prime customers even in this remote village. A big draw for transplanted teachers is adventure travel during Alaska's amazing sun-never-setting summer.

This school was full of warm, enthusiastic kids, with dedicated and caring teachers. But it's important to explain what is going on in these classrooms. The science teacher indicated that very little learning took place outdoors—in a world of sustenance. The middle school math class was working on crossword puzzles requiring students to come up with the nine-letter word for "Polygons with similar shapes but different sizes." Language arts adhered to standard curriculum. As one regional educator explained, "Our high school kids have to read Chaucer. I don't have anything against Chaucer, but that isn't something they find interesting." During my visit, I saw no sign of education aligned with tribal life and heritage.

With ESSA opening the door to a waiver, Alaska could move to performance-based assessments. They could unleash the bright Tuntutuliak kids on challenges like designing wind power with parts picked from the junk strewn across their village. Use math and science to improve fishing and hunting strategies. Invent cost-effective ways to provide units with heating or indoor plumbing. Create ways to help wean their communities off of drugs and alcohol. Critically analyze works written in their native language. I can't predict what Alaska will do, but I was encouraged to receive this note from a senior official who attended an *MLTS* community screening:

> And, yes, I did go to the film on Sunday and it had a very big impact on me. The film, along with my current experiences in canceling our assessment, have really shaken my confidence that we are on the right track in this country in terms of the top-down, standardized, homogenized, rule-driven system of public education. I have the very highest confidence and faith in our educators, but they are working within a system that is, I'm afraid, prioritizing the wrong things. I could go on and on. I won't. In short, the film rattled me as an educational leader and as a mother. I don't know what I'm going to do about that, but I am thankful for it and to you.

During this school year, my experiences with native communities fit a pattern. On average, native kids perform poorly on standardized tests, often described as their state's "poorest-performing subsegment." But in Alaska, Arizona, the Dakotas, Hawai'i, Kansas, and Oklahoma, I learned how native kids excel in collaboration, creative problem solving, and hands-on learning. Are their test scores low because they lack aptitude? Or do poor scores reflect tests that are distant from their culture, upbringing, and interests? Is the problem the kids, or is the problem the tests?

For native kids, education is the gift that keeps on taking. They're fed a steady diet of Western-culture-infused curriculum and tested on skills not aligned with life or their strengths. There are bright spots. In Oklahoma, 20% of their 650,000 school kids are of native descent, and their educators reflect this diversity—some 50 superintendents, 128 principals, 110 counselors, and over 3,500 teachers are of native descent. Many Oklahoma schools offer

Indian languages (e.g., Choctaw) as a foreign language option. But nationally we're not going far enough in connecting kids with place-based and culture-based learning aligned with the opportunities of the twenty-first century.

St. Louis, Missouri—To see inspired learning at scale, come to the FIRST Robotics championship. FIRST (For Inspiration and Recognition of Science and Technology) was started by Dean Kamen, who dropped out of Worcester Polytechnic Institute to invent full-time. He now holds 440 patents for inventions as far-ranging as the Segway personal transporter, insulin pumps, an all-terrain electric wheelchair, Stirling engines, and water purification equipment. Fittingly, Dean's father was an illustrator for *Mad, Weird Science*. As he dashes between meetings, Kamen looks more like a casino owner than a white-lab-coat inventor. In 1989, he wanted to celebrate science and technology in high schools—make it cool to be a nerd—with these guiding principles:

> It's after school, not in school. It's aspirational, not required. You don't get quizzes and tests, you go into competitions and get trophies and letters. You don't have teachers, you have coaches. You nurture, you don't judge. You create teamwork between all the participants. We justify sports for teamwork but why, when we do it in the classroom, do we call it cheating?

Along the way, Kamen teamed with MIT professor Woodie Flowers, who suggested a robotics competition. Designing robots isn't the end goal; it's a way to get kids excited about STEM. From a modest 1992 start with twenty-five teams in a New Hampshire high school gym, FIRST now encompasses four hundred thousand students from all grade levels, all U.S. states, and all around the world.

A FIRST team consists of a dozen or so kids, supported by adult volunteers. Each January, FIRST releases the ground rules for the

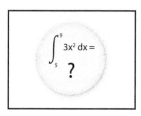

FIGURE 6.2. FIRST Robotics Team Button (reflecting quirky nerd humor!).

coming spring's competition, and teams work countless hours after school and on weekends to design great robots. These agile, intelligent machines physically resemble the base of a miniature military tank. I watched one 125-pound robot collide with another, flip onto its back, and right itself within seconds. Amazing. Keep in mind, we don't teach engineering in high school—they're learning from scratch. On these teams, many competencies are respected—software, hardware, mechanical and electrical design and trouble-shooting, construction, finance, marketing, project management, and good-old keeping everyone happy. FIRST goes far beyond STEM, celebrating the practical and the artistic.

After local rounds all around the world, some twenty thousand kids from forty-two countries come to the St. Louis finals in a mes-merizing celebration of technology and camaraderie. Nerdiness and creativity abound, from team uniforms (e.g., Doctor Spock ears) to creative names (e.g., GearHeads, TeamClutch, Kil-A-Bytes). Teams design and give out clever buttons with their logo. The convention floor has rows of staging booths where teams hang out and pre-pare for the next round. These, too, are conduits for creative signs, posters, and photos. One team's sign was a closed-form integral that, when solved, yielded their team number. When they saw how the smartphone app PhotoMath solved it instantly, they groaned, "Why do we have to do this by hand in math class?"

These robots performed on a playing field that looks like a small indoor-soccer arena with medieval castles at either end. A FIRST team doesn't compete on its own but in conjunction with two other teams, facing off against another grouping of three. In early rounds, teams are randomly assigned to groupings. As teams advance, they get to choose from the "losers" to assemble a strong coalition. A team you compete against early might be your partner later, promoting sportsmanship. As one match began, six industrial-strength robots swing into action—a blue grouping with teams from Kansas, Florida, and Ontario facing a red grouping with teams from Tel Aviv, California, and North Dakota. Balls get hurled, obstacles get navigated, robotic arms get raised to hassle other robots, a few rogue robots dash back and forth navigating ramps, and humans occasionally roll the FIRST equivalent of bowling balls onto the field. Chaos with underlying purpose.

Youth sports are often marred by screaming parents and angry players, but FIRST is chill, reflecting "gracious professionalism." Even mid-contest, teams pause to help others. Kids take pride in their performance but when a contest ends, it's hard to tell winners from losers. FIRST's prestigious awards recognize civic engagement, not point totals. I got goose bumps when 40,000 attendees cheered for a team from one of Nevada's poorest communities that won the Chairman's Award for raising $2 million to bring tech centers to poor communities throughout their state.

FIRST asked me to screen *MLTS* during the championships, and some 350 parents and students showed up. Many attend conventional schools and didn't hold back. One described administrators hassling them for leaving school a few minutes early for robotics. Another commented, "I loved the film. Can you help me make my school bearable?" A seventh-grader had seen Tony's and my book on his dad's bedside table, read it cover to cover, and gave copies to his school's administrators. These kids are thriving in FIRST's PEAK environment, something largely absent during their school day. I encouraged them to make the most of their time outside of school. Be entrepreneurial. Start a company with teammates. Get local organizations to pay you for designing robot-based solutions.

FIRST is fun, launches kids into great careers, and reflects PEAK learning. The question is, why is this just an after-school program for less than 1% of America's students? If school were more like FIRST, we'd have far fewer robotic students. FIRST also underscores the gap in resources available to schools across our country. A FIRST program costs at least $10,000 and requires hundreds of hours of adult support. Affluent schools have ready access to these resources. Many poor schools don't, despite FIRST's deep commitment to social equity. In walking among the twenty thousand participants at the Edward Jones Dome, I saw few black or Hispanic students.

A science teacher who coached an inner-city FIRST team elaborated on this experience. He described his kids as "tenacious, inventive, and capable." His team in St. Louis won its regional against more affluent schools with inherent advantages—funding, prior robotics experience, ringers who have gone to coding summer camps, well-equipped practice facilities, fully functioning subassemblies from prior years, tech-savvy parent volunteers. This inner-city FIRST coach floored me in describing his biggest challenge: a central office that sucked time and energy out of him and his fellow teachers. He had me visualize a building with hundreds of employees who spend short workdays generating bureaucratic requests for teachers in the field. Like most outstanding STEM teachers, he gets weekly offers from other schools. He ended up leaving his school for a less bureaucratic alternative, concluding, "It's heartbreaking to abandon these great kids, but I couldn't stand it anymore."

What happens if our poorest kids don't have access to engaging programs like FIRST? Here in Missouri, look no further than the Hilltop Detention Center in Jackson County. Nationally, facilities like Hilltop educate some 50,000 young kids, almost all African American, Hispanic, or Native American. Hilltop's teachers work with about a hundred teenagers who have crossed enough lines—a felony or a series of misdemeanors—to end up in a detention center. Hilltop is so underresourced that it issued a press release when the Rotary Club donated a few hundred bucks for some shelves and library books. A program like FIRST is beyond their wildest dreams.

Hilltop's teachers came in forty-five minutes early to tell me about their kids. One described a student who was "passionate about learning how to weld, but his school funneled him into college prep courses. It wasn't that he couldn't do the work. It was he didn't want to. And that played out in various ways that led him to jail." A second added, "These kids know what they want to do—things like construction, culinary, medical. They just need a school that helps them get there. Our biggest challenge here is to put school into a real-world setting." These teachers were drawn to Hilltop because they believe in the kids and are grateful that "no one worries about the test scores of these kids, so we have a lot of freedom." For example, one teaches math tied to designing a house, estimating the cost of a trip, and managing credit card debt. These kids' biggest challenges are social and emotional, not academic, but "in regular school, you risk your job if you really engage with kids." A young teacher offered this moving observation:

> Our main goal is to give these kids some hope. They have had a very tough time growing up. We're not talking about Ward and June Cleaver. They've been crapped on so many times by society. They're in pure survival mode. I had to give one of my students a test that showed a pregnant woman in a doctor's office with the question, "What is the setting?" My student answered "Emergency room," which the answer sheet deemed incorrect. What these test designers don't realize is that some of these kids have never been to a doctor's office.

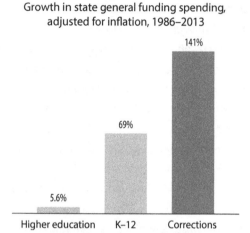

Growth in state general funding spending,
adjusted for inflation, 1986–2013

FIGURE 6.3. Long-term Consequences of Underinvesting in Education. Growth in state general fund spending, adjusted for inflation, 1986–2013. *Source*: This material was created by the Center on Budget and Policy Priorities (www.cbpp.org).

Hanover, New Hampshire—As I traveled, I met people going to great lengths to support young kids in challenging circumstances. Generous, noble acts of love. Teresa Ellis runs Dartmouth's Center for Service with its inspiring mission of preparing students to "lead lives of purpose in the world through engagement in service to others." As a parent with young kids, she makes the considerable sacrifice of commuting daily from Boston's North Shore to Hanover, New Hampshire, for her job. As if her plate isn't already full, she sets aside time to help a young girl living in poverty. Ellis elaborated,

> I have, for the last four years, mentored a young woman. The number of times that she has said to me that her school doesn't think she's very smart just breaks my heart. When I ask her why she says this, she talks to me about the standardized tests she has to take and how she struggles to meet the standards that are defined as "just proficient." She says that if

she is not even proficient on the test, how can she be proficient in life? That's quite a message for someone who is only twelve to have internalized.

Augusta, Maine—The nation's eighty thousand beds for the homeless include twenty at the Bread of Life homeless shelter in Augusta, Maine. For anyone reduced to living on the street or in a homeless shelter, life is hell. A range of circumstances can put someone there—from psychological challenges, to addiction issues, to just plain losing a job with nowhere to turn. Read Richard LeMieux's *Breakfast at Sally's* to appreciate how readily success can turn to homelessness.

One group at Bread of Life was a mother with her three children—ages sixteen, fourteen, and eleven. Like any parent, she has aspirations for her kids and fights fiercely for them in the face of unimaginable challenge. Like most shelters, Bread of Life limits someone's length of stay—six weeks in their case. When you max out, you're either back on your feet, back on the street, or off to a different shelter. Homeless kids are in and out of several shelters and schools each year, destroying continuity with teachers, courses, classmates, clubs, or sports. At Bread of Life, the school bus picks them up in front of the shelter, so other kids know these kids are homeless and, sadly, tease and bully them. Without a computer or even a smartphone, these kids have to schlep to the library for online access. They get screwed every which way from Sunday.

On any given day, some two million school-age children in America are homeless. In a country of rugged individualism, it's one thing to turn our back on struggling adults, something I saw firsthand from a colleague as we were walking in downtown San Francisco. As we passed several homeless people, he told me, "Oh, you just get used to them after a while." Ouch! But in the world's wealthiest nation, can we get used to two million children who spend time each year homeless?

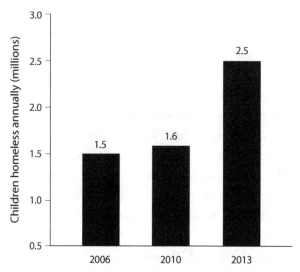

FIGURE 6.4. An Epidemic of Child Homelessness. *Source*: Data from National Center on Family Homelessness at the American Institutes for Research.

In schools that focus on content coverage, it's nearly impossible for a student to switch schools midyear and catch up. Homeless kids are inevitably behind in class, get hammered on exams, struggle to make friends, are bullied, and lose confidence and hope. If schools focused on essential skills tied to real-world projects, it would be easier for a new student to hit the ground running. If report cards were along the lines of Scott Looney's mastery transcript, many homeless kids would do exceptionally well on aspects related to character, receiving an excellent assessment for their "fighting through adversity" skills.

This book is about our K–16 education system, not the pre-K years. That's not from lack of concern—there's only so much I could do on one trip, in one book. As I traveled, though, I saw the impact of the horrendous circumstances in which many children grow up—lacking basic nutrition, housing, or any sense of security. We turn our back on these children and then expect our K–6 teachers to work miracles. When test scores sag, we shouldn't blame the teacher if their students struggle to stay awake for lack of nutrition or are afraid they won't have anywhere to sleep that night.

_____ \\|/ _____

Selma, Alabama—A bridge, a justice, a jarring juxtaposition.

As I made my way to Montgomery, Alabama, I noticed I'd be driving by historic Selma. Having never been there, my first thought was to duck off the highway, explore the city and its historic Edmund Pettus Bridge, and continue on my way. But getting there at night was hardly ideal. I decided to eat the cost of my hotel room booked in Montgomery, spend the night in Selma, and see the bridge the next morning. Upping the ante, I decided to get up before daybreak to watch sunrise from a bridge rich in history.

On my pre-dawn drive to the bridge, I heard a voice on the radio say, "It does not benefit African Americans to get them into the University of Texas where they do not do well, as opposed to having them go to a less-advanced school, a slower-track school where they do well." He continued, "One of the briefs pointed out that most of the black scientists in this country don't come from schools like the University of Texas. They come from lesser schools where they do not feel that they're being pushed ahead in classes that are too fast for them." Being in Alabama, I just assumed this was a story reflecting remnants of southern prejudice.

It wasn't, though. This breaking story was about *Fisher v. The University of Texas at Austin*, an affirmative action case that had made its way to the U.S. Supreme Court for oral arguments on December 9, 2015. The voice belonged to (since deceased) Supreme Court Justice Antonin Scalia, one of America's most powerful men. The case is one in a long series of court battles over the role of affirmative action and race in college admissions.

In 1997, the state of Texas enacted House Bill 588 requiring state colleges, including flagship University of Texas (UT), to admit any applicant who ranks in the top 10% of their high school class. A white student not quite in the top 10% of her class at a high-performing affluent school could be denied admission, despite exceptional SAT and AP scores. "Her" spot might instead go to a Hispanic or black student with subpar scores who graduated in the top 10% of her class at an impoverished high school. Two well-off white students, Abigail Fisher and Rachel Michalewicz, were rejected by UT and filed suit in 2008, arguing that the admissions policy discriminated on the basis of race, in violation of the Equal Protection Clause of the Fourteenth Amendment.

Scalia cited a brief that draws on the work of Richard Sander, a white, Harvard-educated law professor at UCLA. Sander's book *Mismatch: How Affirmative Action Hurts Students It's Intended to Help, and Why Universities Won't Admit It* lays out this argument. When elite universities bend admissions criteria to accept less-qualified minority students, they admit students who—on average—do worse in courses and drop out disproportionately. If these minority students had gone to an unheralded lower-quality college, they'd be more likely to graduate. Match great students with great colleges and lousy students with lousy colleges, he argues, and everyone is better-off.

It's worth noting that our Supreme Court today consists entirely of members who studied law at Harvard or Yale. The only exception in recent decades was Sandra Day O'Connor, who slummed it at Stanford. As judicial scholar Patrick Glen of the Georgetown University Law Center notes, "In essence, a candidate who received his or her legal education in a locale other than Cambridge or New Haven should lower their aspirations . . . if past is prologue, they will have no hope of setting up an office in the Marble Palace."[7] In today's America, only those with degrees from our most elite colleges are qualified to rule on issues affecting mainstream America.

Scalia's words made me sick to my stomach. I would have felt this way on any morning, but this wasn't any morning. The Edmund Pettus Bridge. Named for a former brigadier general of the Confederate Army and Grand Dragon of the Ku Klux Klan. Where civil rights advocates led by Martin Luther King Jr. met at daybreak for their planned march to Alabama's capital to protest insidious tactics preventing blacks from voting. Where police savagely beat protestors on what is now called Bloody Sunday. Where television cameras captured this police brutality with footage that rippled across our nation and generated a groundswell of support for the civil rights movement.

The Pettus Bridge itself is unremarkable. While you can find exquisite facilities and museums at other National Historic Landmarks, the National Voting Rights Museum at the bridge's southern base looks like an abandoned diner. A second building, which in a prior life was a six-car stand-alone garage, features creative artwork on rusted sectional doors. One declares, "Education Is the Key to Control Our Destiny." To the east across US Route 80 is a small park with a few plaques and stone memorials. Suffice it to say, an experience at the Pettus Bridge gets no lift from the physical surroundings. But walking this bridge at daybreak, reflecting on what happened fifty years ago, is powerful.

This day made me question what I was questioning. When I set out in September, I was focused on pedagogy. Surely school could be something more than a place where children are memorizing material they don't care about, won't remember, and won't ever use. If young adults need to be bold and creative in a world brimming with innovation, we can't tolerate education policies that destroy these characteristics. We can't insist on a college degree as a precondition for getting an interview, unless our colleges are better, more affordable, and more accessible.

But what if this issue is deeper? Americans revolted against the British Empire to form a meritocracy, a land where talent and effort—not bloodline—determine success in life. Our Declaration of Independence states, "We hold these truths to be self-evident, that all men are created equal, that they are endowed by their Creator with certain unalienable Rights, that among these are Life, Liberty and the pursuit of Happiness." Sure, we're still a work in progress in going from "all white men are created equal" to "all people, irrespective of race, gender, religion, or sexual orientation, are created equal." But again and again, Americans have worked collectively to fight discrimination, to provide equal opportunity for all. America at its best.

Most would readily agree that discrimination is wrong. But discriminating on the basis of merit is not only tolerated, it's essential. We don't boycott products from Apple Computer because the company refuses to hire inept designers. We don't criticize the Kansas City Symphony for its blatant bias against bad musicians. No one faults the Los Angeles Dodgers—the franchise that had the courage to play Jackie Robinson in 1947—for excluding klutzes from its roster. These organizations succeed by being effective in discriminating on the basis of merit.

Society uses education qualifications as a shortcut to screen people, to evaluate them, to discriminate. It happens every day, in all walks of American life—from cocktail parties to conferences, from OKCupid to LinkedIn. We elevate someone with a Harvard degree, and stack the deck against someone without academic heft. The question is, does this discrimination reflect merit or family station?

For much of our history, quality K–12 education was a free public good and college was affordable. Education equipped kids with relevant skills and sorted them on the basis of merit. But this is no longer true. A recent Jack Kent Cooke Foundation report found that just 3% of the enrollment at our nation's most competitive colleges comes from families in the bottom income quartile.[8] At most elite colleges, as many students come from the society's top 1% as from the bottom 60%.[9] College is by, for, and of the affluent. Kids in poverty lack the advantages of the affluent—the right schools, tutors and test prep, coaches for niche sports, and distinctive community service. They underperform on the gold standard for college admissions, the SAT, which the *Wall Street Journal* termed the Student Affluence Test.[10] Admissions policies heap added advantages on the rich—like preference for legacy and early decision applicants. Without a doubt, money talks when it comes to getting into a top college.

The *Fisher* case highlights what is baked into society's perspective on college—an applicant's qualifications are fairly represented by their numbers (test scores, GPA). A college is somehow bending the rules if it accepts someone with subpar test scores. When colleges make exceptions, it's viewed as one of those things colleges do to field competitive sports teams or check off diversity boxes. But our core assumption is that, in a fair world, kids with lower numbers should be tossed into the reject pile. This assumption is so deeply ingrained that even the "exceptions" admitted to a top college are quick to say they don't belong. And their sense of being an imposter is amply reinforced by classmates, professors, litigious students like Fisher, or Supreme Court justices like Scalia.

We live in a country where our Supreme Court debates whether it's appropriate to bend admissions rules, but skips over whether these are the right rules. Americans trust the Supreme Court's academic elite to rule on who can gain access to . . . the academic elite. We genuflect at the altar of test scores, despite ample evidence that they predict next to nothing. Our forefathers conceived of a Supreme Court with the wisdom to look beyond narrow concerns, but our pedigreed Supreme Court can't see the *silva* for the *ligna*. Not one justice raised the essential question: What criteria should our colleges use in admissions? Should admissions value applicants for their demonstrated ability to fight through adversity to make a positive difference in their world? Or for numbers that tell us more about family circumstance than an applicant's character?

Before heading to Montgomery, I visited Selma High School, whose history encapsulates education in the South. In the mid-1970s, Selma had two segregated public schools, until a court order mandated combining the schools. Amid fears of turbulence, it worked for a couple of decades, and Selma was a poster child for school integration. But that changed in 1990, when a mostly white school board didn't renew the contract of the district's first black superintendent. Tensions grew, in part over a tracking system in the school that created de facto segregation. In just a few weeks, hundreds of white kids fled to lily-white private schools. By 2011 only five white students remained at a school of 1,000. So, the thinking went, build a state-of-the-art new facility, and white kids will return to Selma High School. But they didn't.

Selma High's assistant principal spoke glowingly of Alabama's commissioner of education, Tommy Bice, whom I saw in action later that day. She felt Bice trusted educators to do their job. A few months later, Bice was fired by Governor Robert Bentley. In terms of state governments roiling in controversy, Alabama leads the nation, with a trifecta of clouds hanging over it: a governor facing criminal charges over sexual harassment, a Speaker of the House facing a felony corruption trial, and the Chief Justice of the State Supreme Court facing ethics charges. Just more signs of a country that bears no resemblance to what our forefathers imagined for their future America.

Tough stuff, I know. We treasure the occasional story about a child who climbs out of poverty, graduates from a prestigious university, and goes on to success. Since it's possible for a handful, we cling to the view that nothing is broken in America. But it is. Education has become the modern American caste system. We fuzz up the issue in a sea of statistics about test-score gaps, suggesting that social inequity is a classroom issue. We bemoan the achievement gap but dwell on the wrong "achievement" and the wrong "gap." Achievement should be based on challenging real-world problems, not standardized tests that amount to little more than timed performance on crossword puzzles and sudoku. The gap we need to face is how much more we spend to educate our rich children than our poor. We can test until the cows come home, and we won't begin to bring meaningful equity to our youth. As an educator in the Midwest noted, "If a cow is starving, we don't weigh it. We feed it."

Human Potential

Is the purpose of school to develop human potential or to rank it? The answer seems obvious. Clearly, children attend school to find their talents and interests, develop their potential, and get the education required to lead fulfilling and responsible lives. Can there be any doubt about this?

Yes. Based on my travels, I believe that the purpose of school today in America is to rank potential, not develop it. Worse, schools rank potential on the basis of inconsequential proficiencies, in ways that provide outsized advantage to the affluent. This has consequences. Despite our "No Child Left Behind" aspirations, we're leaving millions behind in order to produce data used to rank students, schools, districts, and states.

Imagine you're advising a powerful country on their strategy for excelling in athletics. This country's preeminent goal is to dominate the Summer Olympics, a spectacular ensemble of hundreds of events. And they're failing. In the last games, they ranked fortieth, trailing even tiny Malta and Slovakia. It's not for lack of effort. Their youth spend more time training than kids in any other country and vie fiercely for admission to prestigious, selective training academies. This country is consumed by Olympic performance.

When you visit your first academy, you see athletes throwing heavy rocks. You assume it's a warm-up exercise, but it goes on all day, for every athlete. Officials explain that their training programs revolve around an event called the Stone Throw. Why? With pride, they explain that their country won the gold, silver, and bronze Olympic Stone Throwing medals in 1906. Although the event was subsequently discontinued, their sports statisticians have done numerous studies showing that stone-throwing performance is correlated with overall athletic ability. Distances can be readily measured, making it easy to rank budding athletes and monitor progress. These numbers provide an objective basis for determining who gains admission to their elite academies. They note an added benefit—young kids are bored to tears throwing stones, so this training regimen builds grit.

No country does this in athletics. But is this what we do in our schools? Are standardized tests the academic equivalent of stone throwing? Are we turning off millions of high-potential athletes across a wide range of sports, as we single out a few who excel on something pretty darn irrelevant? Are we discouraging kids from inventing new sports? Keep this metaphor in mind as we journey across America. Does school develop human potential or rank it?

Salt Lake City, Utah—Dyslexics struggle mightily in school, yet many knock the ball out of the park in life. For any kid, school is a daily regimen of digesting written material quickly, committing it to memory, and drawing on it to navigate timed exams. But if the words or arithmetic expressions on a page look jumbled, these tests are unadulterated hell. Every school day attacks a dyslexic's sense of worth.

Utah's Shellie Burrow is a fierce advocate for kids with learning challenges. She founded the SAIL (Solutions for Advanced and Individualized Learning) Academy to help kids who learn differently and pours herself into this mission. She notes a pattern with her kids. Standard schools wait until they are failing and then push them harder to learn conventionally. Burrow observes,

This model consistently sends a message to students that they are broken or somehow substandard. It has deep and lasting impact. I see it in little students and the heartbreaking comments, tears, and acting out. I hear it from adults who spent years in an academic setting that failed them.

Burrow and I talked about the role of timed multiple-choice tests in determining school's winners and losers—tests that are absent in adult life. They anoint a few percent as gifted on the basis of mental agility, not depth of thinking. And there's no evidence the two are correlated. Each year, millions get the message that they are deficient—irrespective of talents that lie outside the realm of bubble tests. Dyslexics get pummeled in this process.

Burrow illuminated ways she innovates with her students. "Each day, these amazing thinkers have big and unique ideas . . . and often bring them up at the most inconvenient times." She sets time aside each day for "Think Tank." As out-of-the-box (and out-of-context) ideas are raised, she adds them to the list for their next Think Tank session. This approach values audacity, without wreaking havoc on class flow. She cited a recent example when a student asked out of the blue, "Can we listen to music during math?" It would be easy to shut down this kid. Instead, this question went into their Think Tank. The next day, they had a vigorous discussion of the impact of music on retention and the relationship between music and math. Further, students developed guidelines for when music can be played during the school day.

Burrow called *MLTS* "the anthem for the dyslexic community." She wasn't surprised to learn that High Tech High, the school featured in *MLTS*, educates a disproportionately high percentage of dyslexics. Everything changes if school is about projects, big ideas, and curiosity. Students get good at making things, coming up with creative ideas, asking thoughtful questions. Accomplishment is reflected by what is produced. No one cares how long it takes a student to read material or if they learn from a YouTube video or classmate. Just like life. Burrow explained that dyslexics thrive in these learning environments, quoting a line from the film: "We all learn in different ways."

Before this year, I hadn't done much public speaking—certainly not daily to large audiences. At my events, I offer to stay as long as anyone wants to talk. And people take me up on it, lingering to share intense personal stories. These few typify what I heard for the nine months.

- A young man, in his early thirties, waited an hour to tell me about his acute shame over not having a high school degree. He manages a local hotel, where he creatively solves problems, collaborates, and communicates. He fights back tears as he relates the impact of hearing the message that these competencies, not credentials, are what matter in life.
- A woman, in her early twenties, waited ninety minutes to tell me that she got addicted to drugs in high school and struggled for years. Two years ago, she turned her life around at a rehab center that helped her with self-direction, agency, problem solving, communication, and collaboration. She said, "If my school had this focus, I doubt if I would have turned to drugs. I'd have six years of my life back." She wondered if our education model is contributing to our nation's drug-addiction epidemic.
- A mother, daughter in tow, asks for advice on getting her thirteen-year-old into either Harvard or Stanford, explaining that her "gifted" child has already skipped two grades. During the conversation, the little girl burst into tears. The mother begins to sob when asked, "Is any college acceptance, no matter how prestigious, worth this?"

- A group of five teachers explain that their principal checks daily to make sure they're on the specified page of the text. If not, they're reprimanded, even humiliated. They beg for suggestions about how to change their environment.

- A woman talks about her two daughters, explaining that one tested as gifted, with an IQ of 146, while the other's IQ of 80 sent her to special ed. She pushed her "gifted" child hard. This daughter, at age twenty-four, had a breakdown that led to her being committed to a mental institution. Her other child is now a motivational speaker. "You never know," she said softly, and disappeared into the crowd.

--- ⋰⎪⁄⋰ ---

Little Rock and Fort Smith, Arkansas—Little Rock is home to eSTEM High, fueled by Noble Impact's education entrepreneurship program. Noble's leaders—founders Steve Clark and Chad Williamson and CEO Eric Wilson—are experts in entrepreneurship, purpose-driven education, and scalability. Clark started a packaging and logistics business twenty-five years ago, which grew substantially with a boost from a little customer called Wal-Mart. He doubled down with smart investments in start-ups. Clark traces his passion for reimagining education to an experience he had with his son.

> I have a son Andy and I was having a conversation with him about a particular class. And he was just struggling. He said to me, "Dad, it's really just not worth my time. I don't understand why I need to be in this class." And, basically, he concluded the conversation by saying, "If there's no purpose, there's no reason to study this." From a dad's perspective, I was tempted to scold, to preach. But I took that opportunity to reflect, and I was just curious on whether or not I was listening to the insights of a lazy sixteen-year-old or the insights of a generation.

Noble emphasizes student-driven learning, with teachers there to "help them navigate opportunities, without steering the ship." Adults help students "to believe in their potential" and to find "meaning in their lives." Their kids build essential skills by tackling important community problems or starting new organizations. They present accomplishments publicly and get school credit for this work. I met one young eleventh-grader who showed me her stunning digital portfolio of film work, with the theme of inspiring action in her community. PEAK. Kids here were on fire with questions—about school, summer jobs, careers, how to start new initiatives—and most went to a screening of *MLTS* that evening. One tenth-grader e-mailed me at 3:00 a.m., sharing his blog post about the importance of relevant, student-driven learning. Another young woman sent an e-mail that concluded with, "Please don't stop what you're doing. I speak on behalf of every high school student. They deserve to love what they do." These were the notes that made every day of my trip an honor.

Fort Smith, a city of eighty-five thousand, has lost the companies that once made it a thriving manufacturing hub. The downtown area is marked by a number of boarded-up motels and hotels. In a visit to their Boys and Girls Club, I found energized kids playing sports, working on school stuff, and locked into animated conversation. These Fort Smith kids were almost all middle school African American kids from the poorest section of Fort Smith. This organization is one of some two thousand Boys and Girls Club of America centers that provide safety, support, and education to four million American kids.

The afternoon's main attraction was a presentation by Trish Flanagan, who was starting a new high school, the Future School. She asked thirty middle school kids, "What careers or professions are you interested in?" Every hand went up. When I was their age, my answer would have been "major league pitcher," so I expected sports and entertainment answers. But these kids responded

"Surgeon," "Geologist," "Computer programmer," "Journalist." Dying to understand more, I tried to get a sense of whether their parents were in these professions. Not even close. Maybe they'd recently participated in a career exploration day. Nope. They were just motivated, curious kids wanting to do something in life.

Flanagan introduced me briefly to the group, mentioning my technology background. When her talk ended, five kids dashed over to talk to me about computer programming. A young girl related how she had learned basic programming skills through Minecraft. A fellow online forum participant told her that she will excel at coding, something that leads to great jobs. Her enthusiasm spread to her friends. We talked about ways they might identify a problem in their community and create a coding-based solution. I suggested they get help from a computer science professor at the University of Arkansas, Fort Smith. They were skeptical, but I assured them they could pull this off. After a quick iPhone Google search, I gave them the contact information for the department chair as they boarded their bus to depart. I hope they gave it a shot. Even more, I hope their dreams become more, not less, attainable with help from people like Flanagan and Clark, himself a Fort Smith native and resident. These kids will decide Fort Smith's future. As for what motivates Flanagan to put in seventy hours a week to start a school, she offered, "We don't need schools that make kids memorize the names of planets. We need schools that inspire kids to find new planets."

Williamsburg, Virginia—Ellen Stofan is the kind of rock star our country needs. She holds a PhD in geology, or what she calls "rocks." This daughter of a NASA engineer saw her first rocket launch at age four. Like many young kids, she loved science. Unlike many, she retained this love. By age ten, she knew she wanted to study space as a scientist, rather than be in space as an astronaut. She recalls the joy when she realized this pursuit could become her career. She went on to be NASA's chief scientist.

As part of her NASA responsibilities, Stofan visits schools to talk to kids about STEM careers. Sitting next to her on a panel at the College of William & Mary, I saw her inspire a room of adults. I can only imagine her impact on students. She brings passion for unlocking opportunity: "We face such big problems as a society. How can we hope to solve them if some 60% of our population—young women and students of color—are largely shut out of fields that enable them to make a big difference?" Stofan's life mission is to effect change in an education system that shuts many out of inspiring STEM careers.

Stofan has the most thought-provoking views on girls and STEM. Most young girls are enthusiastic about science in elementary school but seldom pursue STEM careers. She stresses the importance of telling the stories of women in science. Curie, Hopper, and Goodall need to be as familiar as Einstein, Newton, and Da Vinci. She notes, "Science is so much fun, but we make it boring. We make it about rote memorization. When I ask kids about what they're learning, they parrot back definitions like 'mitochondrion is the workhorse of the cell.' They've completely lost the wonder." She notes an encouraging trend she's seeing when STEM courses have real purpose (e.g., Engineering for Sustainability, Engineering for Bringing Power to the Third World). More women participate. She explains, "Young women are far more interested in pursuing STEM as a means to solving big, challenging problems." Yet most schools teach STEM through sterile content (e.g., calculus, thermodynamics, organic chemistry).

Stofan's views intrigued me in the context of hearing from college admissions officers that if applications were gender blind, some 60–75% of their entering class would be female. On average, high school girls dramatically outperform boys and choose their college majors from positions of strength. Perhaps intellectually advanced young women prefer courses with authentic challenge (e.g., diving into great works of literature) over curiosity-deadening STEM courses. As some opt out of STEM, those who remain feel increasingly isolated, triggering a vicious cycle. Might it be possible to elevate learning for all, while drawing in more women, by instilling STEM education with purpose and real-world applicability?

The Rich and the Poor, California—California is the global epicenter of entrepreneurs and venture capitalists. Until recently, though, they steered clear of education—viewing it as a small market better left to nonprofits. But the landscape has changed. Since 2011, billions of dollars have been invested in ed-tech companies. Some will succeed, although many are yawners simply digitizing the legacy world of flashcards, study guides, and learning management systems.

Khan Academy (KA) is an online education giant, with tens of millions of users. In 2006, Sal Khan recorded a few YouTube lessons for a niece struggling with a math lesson. She shared them with friends, and it took off. With pedagogy based on short video lectures and multiple-choice quizzes, KA now spans math, physics, chemistry, biology, economics, computing, and history. If it were a for-profit company, KA would be worth several billion dollars, but Sal is motivated by cause, not cash.

When I met Sal in 2013, he was already a national figure. He'd gotten a bear hug and funding from Bill Gates, who promoted KA as the future of education. A world of lectures, laptops, and quizzes— replacing classes, teachers, and peer-to-peer engagement. Big data helping students navigate a rat's maze of personalized learning. In our first conversation, I expressed skepticism that meaningful learning comes from this approach. Expecting to be blown off, we had a great discussion about his *One World Schoolhouse* book, his dismal experience with lectures at MIT, and his education views.

Our conversation turned to how to build on KA's traction. Start a lab school where kids take on open-ended meaningful challenges, drawing occasionally on KA for "just in time" learning. Complement KA's library of lectures on low-level procedures with a repository of meaningful math-based challenges, something I called "Khan Exploratorium." Establish a center—the Bell Labs of education—to spark global innovation.

To bring an Exploratorium to life, I described the best math challenge I've encountered, which was in a middle school social studies class. Huh? Students were challenged to come up with ways to predict the world's population in the year 2100. Work alone or in small teams. Use any available resources. Compute it with paper and pencil, calculator, or spreadsheet, or write your own code (some did!). Present your work to classmates, addressing their questions. When others present, ask informed questions and offer constructive suggestions. Then, discuss the implications of each projected population (which ranged from 0 to 30 billion) for their future world. Unlike the math that kids do in school, this problem requires creativity. There's no right answer. Kids learn point concepts (curve fitting, extrapolation, eigenvalues) in a meaningful context. Often, "bad" math students thrive, while "gifted" math students flounder. In contrast, our current math track has nothing to do with the creativity and conceptualization that make for a great mathematician. Students never learn to apply math to real-world challenges. Everything would be different if our K–12 schools taught math that matters, instead of symbolic arithmetic.

Although I didn't expect to hear from Sal again, he reached out a few months later to discuss plans for an R&D initiative. I committed support and helped him raise money from others. Subsequently, though, his organization hadn't exactly erred on the side of overcommunicating, so I was anxious for an update. On his favored "walk and talk" through the neighborhood, he reported on the growing number of users of Khan Academy, their new online test-prep offering, and progress on a lab school immersing Silicon Valley kids in open-ended challenges. But other than completing some legal work, no progress on the challenge of scaling insights from this "lab" to schools around the world.

On my way to Sacramento, I reflected on why Sal's outstanding team had prioritized on test prep (SAT, MCAT, GMAT) over real innovation. I thought back to our first conversation. "Sal, why produce hundreds of lectures teaching kids how to do integrals by hand? They watch your video on a device that performs these operations instantly, perfectly. Let computers do the mechanics and teach kids how to solve real problems using math—something school never gets to. Help our kids leverage technology, not compete against it." To which a staff member offered, "We need to focus on where today's market is"—an odd priority for a nonprofit aspiring to improve education.

When I met Dr. Darryl Adams, superintendent of the Coachella Valley Unified school district, his first words were, "My district is the second-poorest in the United States." When I asked which is the poorest, he replied, "I don't know, and I'm sure glad it's not mine." Adams started life as a musician and still performs in clubs and at education events.

> After college, I was into the creative process around music. I was in a band in Memphis, six poor black boys got lucky with a record deal that made us rich and famous for five or six years. Xavion. Our most popular song: *Eat Your Heart Out*. We opened for Hall & Oates on their national tour, and lived that rock 'n' roll lifestyle for a while. But it didn't last. After the band broke up, I came to Los Angeles seeking fame and fortune, which didn't work out. But my music credential let me start teaching, and I loved it.

In a district just thirty miles west of Palm Springs, 100% of Darryl's students live in poverty—many in trailer homes or abandoned railroad cars, or homeless. His 20,000 students struggle daily to survive. Families typically earn less than $1,000 per month and can't afford food, let alone a family computer. In a district with more square miles than Rhode Island, many kids lack Internet coverage outside of school. Adams proposed equipping all students with tablets and giving them 24/7 WiFi access. How? "Why can't we put routers on our 100 school buses and park them at night in neighborhoods? At first they thought I was crazy but then they said 'OK.' " He added, with a laugh, "Hey, I'll put a WiFi router on a pigeon if it helps my students." Against long odds, the community passed a $45 million school bond in 2012 to fund a Mobile Learning Initiative. Now, buses park each night in neighborhoods, giving students access to online resources to help with their work. The concerns voiced about vandalism? No issues to date.

Adams's district buzzes with informed innovation. Their "Full STEAM Ahead" initiative helps students find career pathways. "We focus on careers where there's a need. We're making education relevant. Our students are learning about aviation, environmental science, health care, drones, construction, electronics." Adams is persuasive in enlisting the support of local businesses. He somehow convinced a company to donate a Gulfstream 2 jet to his Aviation Academy. His students can take flying lessons and Adams quipped, "I hope I get to fly in it someday." He's investing heavily to "help our teachers understand the importance of helping students learn to use these devices as a tool to create things—articles, essays, movies, music, blogs, science experiments. We want teachers to help students decipher, analyze, dissect, and create, to do research, to get access to information, to solve problems."

Adams offers cogent views on testing. "It's truly folly to use only one measure to decide if a school is good. We know some students don't test well but they can out-create you or out-talk you. Also, are they learning what they want to learn? Why are we testing something that's not relevant to their lives?" He points out that

Common Core was rushed into schools to test kids and compare scores. "We're setting ourselves up for problems. We have a lot of other skills to cover: life skills, character, citizenship." He adds, "I will battle them to the end of time; I'm not playing that game."

Coachella's results are encouraging. Graduation rates increased to 84%, up from 69% when Adams became superintendent in 2011. About 40% go on to four-year colleges, 40% go to community college, and 20% go into the workforce. Adams commented, "We've cut the dropout rate in half. Go talk to the kids. They are learning, growing, and creating like never before." Adams is deeply grateful that Coachella supports his "innovative servant style of leadership."

Asked in 2016 what he'd do if he were secretary of education, Adams remarked, "I would replicate what we've done here. Start with literacy and then focus on the passion that they want to fill their life with. I would have career academies that help students create jobs that don't yet exist. I'd give more attention to character and citizenship." He adds, "There's a lot of focus on charter schools with Washington, D.C., policy, but I don't see many public school people there. We're showing what public schools can do. There are innovative and creative people out there that sometimes get limited by an old way of thinking. Let's create a new system."

During my travels, I kept coming back to the issues of technology, curriculum, human potential, and social equity. Sal Khan is dedicated to giving all kids—rich and poor—free access to education resources. But across America, I didn't find Khan Academy in middle- and low- income schools. Most hadn't heard of it. I did find plenty of well-off kids using it to race their way to a more impressive college application.

Silicon Valley is home to many of our nation's top 1% in power and influence. People there make piles of money through creativity, innovation, and acumen in leveraging resources. Coffee shops are peppered with conversation about the looming impact of artificial intelligence. They ought to be first to recognize that ubiquitous smartphones change what children need to learn. Then there's Darryl Adams. When it comes to academic pedigree, net worth, board seats, and political access, Darryl can't come close to Silicon Valley's movers and shakers. Yet this musician-turned-educator in dirt-poor Coachella has a far more informed view of the role of technology in education than most Silicon Valley thought-leaders.

Maybe kids desperately seeking a way out of poverty have needs different from those of affluent kids with a safety net bigger than the San Francisco Bay. But here's the rub. Darryl doesn't determine U.S. education policy. He doesn't have the ear of leading politicians. He doesn't weigh in on national policies and math standards. Our upper echelon influences not only what their kids get tutored on *but* what Darryl's kids have to study to graduate, how his teachers are evaluated, and whether his kids escape from their trailer park to create a better life.

Should Silicon Valley's priority be helping kids master math they'll never use, just to look more attractive to college admissions officers? Or should it fight for what its culture stands for: creativity, audacity, leveraging the power of technology, and empowering futures?

Boys Town, Nebraska—The very first Super Bowl, retroactively called Super Bowl I, was played in 1967. The Super Bowl is about the only time any of us ever use those Roman numerals we studied in grades III through VI. Super Bowl 50 (they finally gave up the Roman numeral ghost) only had II or III good plays. For most viewers, the commercials were the highlight. But not for Boys Town.

In 1917, a young priest named Father Edward Flanagan was helping the homeless in Omaha and believed there had to be a better way. He borrowed $90, rented a boardinghouse, and set up Father Flanagan's Home for Boys. He welcomed boys of all races and religions. Within a few months, one hundred boys were living there. He had to move from Omaha, though, since having a home for kids of mixed races and religions was controversial in 1917. Four years later, he purchased Overlook Farms, twelve miles west of downtown. Over time, the facility grew to encompass a school, dormitories, and administration buildings. In 1936, it officially became Boys Town, Nebraska.

Flanagan was a man of conviction. The Ku Klux Klan threatened to burn down his facility since it was housing black and Jewish kids. Flanagan asked, "What color is a person's soul?" At a time when he was financially desperate, a donor offered $1 million with the stipulation that he turn away all non-Catholics. Flanagan turned down the money, not the kids. He often remarked, "There are no bad boys. There is only bad environment, bad training, bad example, bad thinking."

Father Steven Boes is the driving force behind an innovative and growing Boys Town. He described our foster care system as "the biggest failed social system in America," calling it a real, live Hotel California ("but you can never leave") for millions of kids desperate for help. The system offers financial incentives to keep beds full, not to help kids gain the skills and confidence to be independent. He's active in trying to rewrite child welfare laws, including directing more resources to prevention and parent education.

Fr. Boes described the kids that Boys Town helps: kids living in constant danger, subjected to physical and emotional abuse, and lacking basic food, clothing, and housing. Then he got specific. Shaquil Barrett, a 2010 graduate of Boys Town, competed in the Super Bowl we watched the night before. Barrett grew up in East Baltimore, a tough neighborhood where it's easy to get into trouble. The family's father encouraged Shaquil to consider Boys Town. After being robbed on the street, Shaquil decided to go. Keep in mind that his dad is a football coach who couldn't afford travel to Nebraska. He was willing to say goodbye to his son, give up his team's best player, and miss any chance to watch his son's games. An amazing, selfless father.

Boys Town athletic programs teach kids about "competing with character"—the social and emotional skills needed to perform at the highest levels. And that's what Barrett demonstrated after completing Boys Town. He started at the University of Nebraska, Omaha, which dropped its football program while he was there. He then competed at Colorado State but wasn't one of the 256 players selected in the 2014 NFL draft. He tried out with the Denver Broncos, was cut, clawed his way onto the practice team, and then made the 53-player roster for the 2015 season. He moved to a starting position midseason on a team that ended up winning it all. So Super Bowl 50 featured a Boys Town alum carrying the torch for this great organization—an alum with a Super Bowl ring that millions of his Boys Town "brothers" take pride in.

Since Fr. Boes became its head in 2005, Boys Town has grown to twelve facilities across the country supporting thirty-two thousand boys and, since 1985, girls. Each site offers group homes, in-home family services, foster care, parenting classes, and behavioral health services. They've built a national research hospital and support an R&D initiative to identify and refine best practices. Their Innovative Family Home Program supports kids living in homes with married couples trained to be "family-teachers" and now reaches hundreds of thousands of people where they live. Boes is scaling impact.

Fr. Boes gave me the Boys Town book *Teaching Social Skills to Youth: A Step-by-Step Guide to 182 Basic to Complex Skills*. It offers lessons in how to communicate respectfully to adults, handle emotions, manage a project, and 179 other useful life skills. I turned to a random page—"Boredom." Ironic. Boes explained that academics at Boys Town are viewed as a means to acquiring important life skills, noting, "It's the social and emotional skills, not algebra, that help young adults become contributing members of their community." Boys Town trusts students to lead and govern their community. Students form their own government and elect a mayor, a council, and commissioners. They set policies on things like discipline. They are treated with respect and rise to expectations. Just like Shaquil Barrett.

Nashville, Tennessee—Serial entrepreneur Hal Cato is the CEO of Thistle Farms, a thriving Nashville organization with the motto "Love Heals." Thistle designs, manufactures, and sells body lotion, scented candles, face cream, and quilts. They've sold to thirty thousand customers to date, generating several million dollars of annual revenue, with products available on Amazon and at Whole Foods around the country. They recently opened a restaurant, with the mission of creating jobs and serving as a community hub for events.

OK, I've dealt with a lot of start-ups, so why was I impressed with Thistle Farms? Well, it's staffed entirely by women struggling to overcome their histories. Most, Cato explains, were ignored and abused when they were young, passed around and sexually abused in foster care, hit the street at the age of fifteen or sixteen as prostitutes, and went down the path of drugs and crime. Many have served time in state prison; I met one with eighty-six prior arrests. The other common denominator? Thistle Farms is helping them get their lives on track, with the opportunity to acquire important life skills as part of the growing Thistle Farm organization.

One employee told me she dropped out of high school two months before the end of her senior year, unable to read. When asked how much she was learning at Thistle Farms, she said, "More in a month than I ever learned in school." I complimented one woman for being so articulate. Fearless, she asked, "What does 'articulate' mean?" Regarding the impact of school on these women, Cato put it so well: "They've been told their whole lives what they're bad at. They carry this with them forever." Thistle's

lead candle-scent designer works long and hard hours as she creates their portfolio of stunning fragrances. Before Thistle Farms, she
had served time in jail for the crime of being a crystal meth chef.
Her "Breaking Good" story shows the fine line between a criminal
and a world-class chemist.

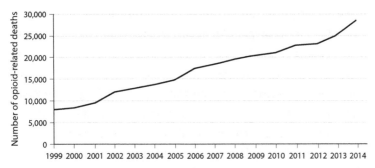

FIGURE 7.1. An Epidemic of Opioid Use. *Source*: Data from Centers for
Disease Control and Prevention.

Portland, Oregon—Twenty-five years ago, Ed Blackburn joined
Portland's Central City Concern (CCC), an organization helping the
homeless, addicted, and mentally challenged. He started as the director of their detox center and progressed to CEO in 2008. Under
his leadership, CCC has more than doubled, growing to 800 employees with an annual budget of $65 million. Its world-class medi-
cal centers attract top doctors from all over the world. They own
90 units of family housing, with another 70 under construction.
They recruit exceptional staff for key roles in management and
fund-raising. Their reputation for excellence attracts donors, partners, expert personnel, and clients. Success begets success. Del-
egations visit from all over the world to learn more about CCC's
innovative model. Fittingly, the Dalai Lama presented Blackburn
with the Unsung Heroes of Compassion Award.

During our conversation, Blackburn kept returning to education. About half of his 800 employees are former patients or residents, and Blackburn views CCC employment as a form of "school." Employees gain essential skills while acquiring expertise in service industries, construction, computer programming, and data analytics. Their caseworkers help place CCC members in jobs with some 250 regional employers. Their annual Education Fair brings in a dozen colleges to explain offerings and financial aid options, with support from CCC's burgeoning scholarship program. He chafed for years under a requirement to train his personnel on diversity issues with prescribed, boring video lectures—"education at its worst." CCC completely reinvented diversity training by creating its Diversity Olympics, an explosion of events, teams, and diversity immersion.

CCC educates the parents in their housing units about how to best help their kids move forward. Blackburn relates, "With many parents, you can see the lights going on, as they relate their problems as adults to childhood issues around school and family." CCC is a residency site for the Oregon Health Sciences University, and residents often tell Blackburn, "This is why I entered the medical profession." These residents learn medical skills through practice and gain a deep understanding of homelessness, addiction, and incarceration.

Blackburn, a firm believer in entrepreneurial community service, created CCC's Community Volunteer Corps. Rather than asking others for a hand-out, CCC members help other Portland nonprofits identify and define problems, then work in teams to create and implement solutions. Blackburn describes this as "Adult Montessori School." Those completing the program—almost all do—participate in a graduation that's a big deal, with family and friends coming to celebrate their accomplishment. Many tell Blackburn, "This is the first thing I've ever graduated from in my life."

A big issue for homeless shelters is dealing with gnarly bedbugs, something CCC has turned into a business opportunity. In 2009,

CCC needed to buy 220 beds and looked for bedbug-resistant offerings. Finding none, they worked with a local steel fabricator and mattress manufacturer to design a bed they now sell on their website. Annual revenue exceeds $2 million, while employees develop valuable skills. Sarah, who had a menial job at CCC, approached Blackburn with insights about improving operations. She now has a full-time senior role and is working at night to get her business degree. Given the success of the bedbug business, they started a coffee business, selling their product in twenty-one states. Blackburn said, "Good coffee, good cause."

Blackburn went out of his way to talk about his brother, a high school English teacher who ran into trouble with his school board. The board specified exactly which books all students had to read, but Blackburn's brother opted to help his students find books they'd like. This went extraordinarily well for the students, but it didn't end well for the brother. Blackburn's parting comment to me was that life is all about respecting human dignity, motivation, and choice. He pointed to CCC's mission statement—"Helping people achieve self-sufficiency."

During my official visit, I couldn't interview CCC patients due to privacy issues. Understandable. But after my meetings, I hung around outside and talked to a few as they passed by. To a person, they credited CCC for giving them the skills and conviction to move forward in life. One described school as where he stopped believing in himself. Another said, "CCC gave me hope, which was missing in my life for a long, long time." A young woman described herself as "the perfect high school student"—honor roll, Homecoming queen, president of two clubs, and accepted by a top university. Growing up, her mother managed her life. Once in college, things fell apart—alcohol, wild parties, frequent hookups, weekly trips to the psychiatric counseling office, and drugs. In tears, she described how desperately she tried to fill the void from "never feeling quite good enough."

State Senator Arnie Roblan and State Representative Marga-
ret Doherty chair Oregon's education committee. Both had been
teachers earlier in their careers. They spoke eloquently about how
NCLB had turned Oregon's Department of Education into a compliance agency, driving creativity and innovation out of school. They
were passionate about an elevated role for hands-on learning. Roblan took joy in sharing his barometer story:

> A student takes a physics exam with the question, "Show how
> to determine the height of a tall building with the aid of a
> barometer." Her answer: "Go to the top of the building, tie a
> long rope to the barometer, lower it until it hits the ground,
> and measure the rope to determine the height." The student
> gets an F, protests, and receives a second chance. Her re-
> vised answer: "Drop the barometer from the top of the roof.
> Count the seconds it takes to hit the ground. Compute height
> using the formula $h = \frac{1}{2}*a*t^2$." Another F, another protest.
> Her professor reluctantly gives her one last chance, and she
> offers multiple answers. "On a sunny day, measure the ba-
> rometer's height, the length of its shadow, and the length of
> the building's shadow. Use trig to compute height." "Mea-
> sure the height of the barometer and each stair step. Count
> the number of steps. Use the ratios to compute height." A
> third solution involves using the barometer as a weight on a
> pendulum. One last answer: "If all else fails, find the building
> superintendent, and offer them the barometer in exchange
> for telling you the building's height." When the exasperated
> professor met with her to give her a definitive F, she explains,
> "Of course I know the answer you're looking for, but isn't the
> essence of science coming up with creative alternatives?" She
> walked out, never to return.

Folks at Oregon's Department of Education explained that the
2008 recession caused the department to pull back on innovation

in their schools—both fiscally and attitudinally. With the recession almost a decade behind us, this struck me as odd. If school leaves millions of young adults vulnerable, where's the urgency for change? Shouldn't we fight for schools that prepare students to start a CCC instead of needing one?

We think of schools as places where we learn, and jobs as places where we work. If we're talking about academic content, fair enough. But if we're talking about PEAK learning, that's a different story. Many people are quite capable of learning, just not in school. The right job can be their salvation. Internships, apprenticeships, and entry-level jobs can make or break a young adult's future. Our K–12 schools need to help students create distinctive competencies that translate into fulfilling careers. We've just visited places that support people whose lives have come unglued. While some recover from a spiral of failure, many others don't. For them, school was where their human potential was lost, not found.

Doing (Obsolete) Things Better

Everyone involved with education has the best of intentions. No one wakes up each morning saying, "Hey, what can I do today to ruin the futures of our children and drive our best teachers out of the profession?" We're all doing what we can to help kids succeed. That's the good news.

I find, though, that many people, especially those in positions of influence, strive to "do things better," which in practice amounts to "do obsolete things better." Metaphorically, conventional schools are covered wagons carrying children who need to move rapidly in today's world. "Do things better" leaders seek operational efficiencies from the existing model. They adopt policies equivalent to beating the mules harder and measuring the wagon's speed more frequently. In contrast, "do better things" leaders realize the covered wagon is obsolete and look for modern, high-speed alternatives.

During this year, my meetings with "do things better" leaders helped me understand their perspective. They invariably have impeccable academic backgrounds. School worked for them, helping them hone the hoop-jumping skills that got them to the top of a bureaucracy. They believe deeply in academics and college's indispensable role. Throughout their successful careers, they've driven organization progress with a top-down metrics-driven approach. Manage people's actions through policies and procedures, seek incremental gain, minimize risk. This is what managers of the bureaucracy do.

This book is about courageous educators daring to do better things. People who don't project their own values onto their students but put in place conditions that empower thriving students to discover and achieve their own definition of success. Transformational leaders view themselves as partners in learning, supporting and trusting teachers in the classroom. But to fully appreciate them, we need to walk in the shoes of a few "do things better" policymakers and see why well-intentioned policies go awry. Let's start at the top.

Washington, D.C.—My original plan for this trip had our nation's capital as my last stop. After visiting all fifty states, I'd meet with policymakers in the White House, Senate, House, and Department of Education, hoping some would be interested. My schedule changed abruptly, though, when I was invited to an Obama White House Summit on next-generation high schools. The detour seemed all the more worthwhile when Bob Wise, the dynamic head of the Alliance for Excellent Education and former governor of West Virginia, asked me to show *MLTS* excerpts at the event's opening night reception and be part of a panel addressing the urgency for reimagining school. Before I dive in, you should know that I was an all-in volunteer for Barack Obama in 2007–8. In 2012, the president appointed me to represent the United States at the 2012 United Nations General Assembly, where I focused on education and youth entrepreneurship. So my concerns about federal policies don't come from knee-jerk antipathy to D.C. or any lack of respect for our forty-fourth president.

President Obama and his talented White House staff worked tirelessly on behalf of America, with lots to show for his presidency. But his education policies did more damage than George W. Bush and his No Child Left Behind (NCLB), which was hard to do.

Obama's Race to the Top (RTTT) made test prep the all-consuming focus of school. In 2015, though, Obama remarked, "Learning is about so much more than just filling in the right bubble. So we're going to work with states, school districts, teachers, and parents to make sure that we're not obsessing about testing." And now the White House was convening an event about reimagining education, convening inspiring pioneers. Maybe it was education's turn for hope and change.

The day's opening speaker was Secretary of Education Dr. John King. After telling his compelling personal story, he addressed the serious issue of the 19% of our kids who drop out of high school, noting that two-thirds of prison inmates are high school dropouts. His plan? "Having more students taking rigorous courses like Algebra II and Chemistry." I struggled to visualize bored teenagers suddenly fired up and ready to go memorize the periodic table. With frequent use of the phrase "false dichotomies," he suggested continuing with our archaic model while reimagining it. Sort of like a secretary of defense talking about modernizing our military through intensive musket training.

King was followed by others who influence U.S. education, with an unlikely issue topping their list of imperatives: calculus. A White House staffer put up a map showing America's "No Calculus Counties," speaking in somber tones about the millions of students deprived of their fundamental right to take calculus. Other well-known policymakers and philanthropists piled on the calculus gap. Leaving no calculus stone unturned, the White House press release on this "first-ever" summit proclaimed, "And we must do more. According to data from the USDOE's Office of Civil Rights, only 50% of high schools in the U.S. offer calculus." The punch line: "We must ensure that all students have access to the full suite of courses that will prepare them for success in the innovation economy."

Now, calculus sounds essential to "success in the innovation economy," a gateway to those enticing jobs of the future. But here's the reality. Other than high school calculus teachers, no adult in America performs by hand the low-level mechanics that comprise high school calculus. The few who use calculus professionally rely on computational resources to compute integrals and derivatives. The biggest calculus issue in our high schools is that too many students take it, not too few, and that it's taught the wrong way.

Calculus does reflect the *true* dichotomy in education. In a world with ready access to computational resources, we need to rethink what's essential. A smartphone can instantly compute integrals and derivatives, yet high school calculus students spend a year drilling on these low-level mechanics, never learning how to apply these tools. When most students take calculus, it's in lieu of statistics— something of great value for career, citizenship, and personal decision making. Organizations don't need employees to do integrals by hand but are desperate for data analytics expertise. In a reimagined math track with ready access to online resources, students would have time to learn probability and statistics, computer programming, estimation, financial literacy, data analytics, decision analysis, algorithm structuring, problem-solving strategies, or digital fabrication. But that's not happening. Students put their smartphones away and drill on the low-level math that populates our standardized tests. Immersed in minutiae, they never get to math's applicability, power, and inherent beauty. To see how far astray we've gone, consider that fewer than 20% of adults in our country use *any* math beyond the basics of middle school.[11] Nearly one-third of American adults prefer cleaning the bathroom to solving a math problem.[12]

People like John King are fighting to help all students, particularly those in poverty. Their policies represent a thoughtful attempt to "do better things." Help our bottom-quartile schools be more like our top-quartile schools. More algebra, chemistry, and calculus. Move kids from slow covered wagons to faster covered wagons. These policies sound good from the podium, but are damaging in a world of powerful machine intelligence.

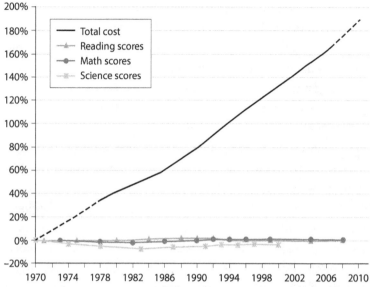

FIGURE 8.1. U.S. Education Policy: Costs and Progress on Its Stated Goal. *Source*: Adapted from National Assessment of Educational Progress.

Near the end of the day and long after the edu-celebrities had left, one public school teacher said to those remaining, "We need to empower our teachers, engage our students, and deliver learning experiences that recognize, and capitalize on, the reality that our students will have digital devices at their fingertips for the rest of their lives." In one simple sentence, she articulated a policy a century ahead of what we heard earlier in the day from those occupying education's commanding heights. They needed to listen to her.

New Orleans, Louisiana—New Orleans is undergoing a post-Katrina charter-school education makeover. John Merrow, long-time and respected journalist for PBS's *NewsHour*, has followed Louisiana education for years. He notes that before Katrina, "the New Orleans school district was an F–, possibly the worst in the country. After a decade of work there, they've lifted it to a C–. But that's about as far as you can go with a strategy based on standardized testing." Merrow chronicles these changes in his compelling documentary *Rebirth: New Orleans*. He observes that New Orleans is following the game plan that Joel Klein implemented in New York City. Over his career, Klein has made many positive contributions to education, including launching the careers of many leaders. But after his test-and-measure strategy stalled in New York City, Klein moved on to become CEO of Amplify, a Category 5 business disaster.

The New Orleans charter school makeover has a strong proponent in John White, Louisiana's superintendent of education. Tall, young, and nattily dressed, White worked in New York City under Joel Klein for the Bloomberg administration from 2006 to 2011, had executive experience with Teach for America (TFA), and came to New Orleans in 2011 to head a recovery school district. When the top spot in Louisiana opened up, he moved to Baton Rouge in 2012 to serve as the state's superintendent of education.

White talked about how "the best teachers I had were coaches" and about the authenticity of youth sports. He related that improved CTE "has my heart the most." As superintendent, he issued the report *Louisiana Believes*, a plan to ensure every Louisiana child is on track to pursue college or a professional career. This blueprint document emphasizes math standards like: "For exponential models, express as a logarithm the solution to $a \bullet b^{ct} = d$, where a, b, c, and d are numbers and the base is 2, 10, or e" and "Interpret the parameters in a linear, quadratic, or exponential function in terms of a context." It would be surprising, very surprising, if any adult in Louisiana uses this math.

Blade Morrish chairs the education committee in Louisiana's state senate. Born and raised in the tiny town of Jennings, he grew up working at his father's hardware store. He left home for college, getting an agriculture degree from McNeese State, expecting to be off to different pastures. To his surprise, he came back to Jennings to run that darn hardware store for thirty years. I guessed that his nickname "Blade" had to do with the hardware store, but in fact he was so skinny when he played college football that his teammates called him "Blade." A leader in his community's chamber of commerce and Rotary, he was elected to the state house in 1996 and to the state senate in 2007. When an opening arose for senate education committee chair, no one wanted it. He points to his balding head, saying, "I was the only one with enough room to write 'fool' on my head." His wife observed that this role brought a glint to his eye. "She called it 'excitement.' I called it 'fear.'" He had a running start in this role, since his wife spent her career in education and reminds him constantly, "All we do anymore is teach to the test."

Morrish made a telling point: "I've always thought that a lot of education issues depend on your personal education experiences—yours and your children's." And he got specific. His nephew graduated from a four-year college, ending up delivering packages for UPS. He quit and completed a two-year career-focused community college program leading to a job he loves as an LNG operator, earning more than $100,000 per year. His daughter got her four-year degree in nursing but didn't like it as a career. She went to a two-year hands-on program to get certified as a pediatric dental hygienist, a career she loves. His brother used his passion for nature and forestry to build a career path selling logging equipment. His constituents don't give a whit about national or international rankings and expect most kids will stay in Louisiana. So the goal of providing them with an education that leads to good jobs is high on Blade's—and his constituents'—priority list.

In many ways, Louisiana typifies what I found in many states: competing agendas. One camp pushes for better test scores, with charter schools as the key. The other senses something fundamentally wrong with our education priorities. Adults in these camps engage in tug-of-war, pulling fiercely against each other. Our kids are the stretched rope in the middle, going nowhere.

Denver, Colorado—Colorado state senator Mike Johnston has impeccable credentials: Yale undergrad, Harvard master's degree in education, Yale Law School degree, two years teaching for TFA in Mississippi, author of *In the Deep Heart's Core*, and six years as a high school principal in northeast Colorado. President Obama and Secretary of Education Arne Duncan tapped him as a key advisor for RTTT. He's a poster child for hedge-fund reformers, garnering prestigious awards from groups like the Democrats for Education Reform.

In 2012, Johnston delivered what someone called "the best education speech ever." His evocative description of his students brought his audience to tears. He talks about his charter school making Colorado history by having 100% of its seniors accepted to four-year colleges. He requires all incoming students to sign pledges committing to college. The progress of each student's "climb to college" is publicly displayed on a personalized cardboard silhouette of a mountain. Each new college acceptance prompts a schoolwide celebration, allowing younger students to take in the euphoria of getting into college.

In his speeches and writings, Johnston attacks a tenure system that "provides no incentive for someone to improve their practice. It provides no accountability to actual student outcomes." When you can hire and fire teachers at will, "you could actually demonstrate amazing results in places where that was never thought possible." Pointing to "the moments of hope that remind us that all things are possible," he describes his legislative fight to expand charters and eliminate tenure, attacking "a policy system in almost every state in this country that's deeply broken. That serves an old set of interests and a wrong set of values." Johnston talks about this growing army of new-wave reformers coming to rescue our kids, drawing parallels to those in Lincoln's cabinet or Martin Luther King's living room. He speaks powerfully of a commitment to truth and hope, dedicated to radically changing what this country is capable of, willing to "hoist America onto its shoulders and carry it across the water where we, like Tashia [one of his students], can say, 'Yes, we can really have that.' "[13]

Johnston may well go on to higher office in his state, perhaps even nationally. Deeply committed to education and public service, he's in the trenches helping kids. By dint of his compelling personality, his students will accomplish the goals he sets for them. His prescription for improving education rests on his past success—more charter schools, better test scores, more kids into college. This simple message appeals, and simple works in America. But in the words of H. L. Mencken, "For every complex problem, there is an answer that is clear, simple, and wrong." And Johnston's clear, simple message misses the mark. Test scores tell us little, charter schools are a mixed bag, and college is a crapshoot. Doing obsolete things better will hardly "carry us across the water."

During my trip, I met with an uber-wealthy hedge-fund reformer who takes his policy cues from Mike Johnston. This financier's large political contributions have enabled him to influence national policy, bending it toward the reformer-accountability agenda. Our conversation was revealing. He was surprised to learn that students generally have no stake in these accountability tests. He wasn't aware that teachers typically get no feedback from these tests to help improve teaching practices. I'd make a large wager that he'd never impose such policies on his children's private schools or on the businesses he finances. But these views have affected millions of others.

The original intent of charter provisions was to foster deep innovation in a few schools, then scale success. Many early charter

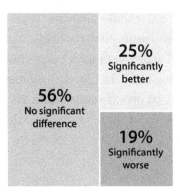

FIGURE 8.2. No Significant Differences between Charter and Public. *Source*: Stanford CREDO 2013 Report.

schools have been remarkable, such as High Tech High, featured in *MLTS*. Charter schools can be effective vehicles for educators experimenting with deep innovation. In some regions, charter schools have injected much-needed energy into large, lethargic school districts. Today, though, many charter schools focus intensely, often ruthlessly, on producing superior test scores. Scores are how they tout success, how they attract their students, and how they raise their money. Innovation is limited to modest tricks of the trade for drill-and-kill classrooms. Many dodge children likely to test poorly. Some, sadly, are fraudulent or abusive. So when you hear the term "charter school," don't jump to conclusions about quality.

The United States faces the pragmatic challenge of elevating learning for all K–12 kids, urgently. Machine intelligence isn't going to wait for us to resolve education infighting. After twenty-five years, charter schools reach just 5% of our students. Even with pedal to the metal, they'll reach just a few percent more of our students each decade. We need to move past distracting either/or issues and start focusing on what, and how, our children learn.

Find ways to let all schools innovate. Take the NCLB strait-jackets off of mainstream public schools. Help educators in a community gain insight from each other's innovations. And to any reformer laying claim to Lincoln's cabinet or MLK's living room: slow down a bit on self-canonization. History's great movements took on causes far more aspirational than doing obsolete things better.

_____ \\|// _____

Topeka, Kansas—In 2012, Kansas governor Sam Brownback signed into law a business tax exemption, assuring voters that the resulting wave of economic growth would offset lost tax revenues. But in the surprise of the century, tax revenue plummeted, causing a massive statewide budget crisis and across-the-board cuts. Brownback's education advisor described this fiscal crisis to me as though it resulted from weather beyond their control. He rationalized that their education system could absorb the cuts, since they've added more new administrative positions than new students over the past decade. I agreed that central office bureaucrats aren't where dollars should be spent, but some back-of-the-envelope math debunked his claim.

To see the impact of state fiscal policy, consider Cynthia Lane, the dynamic superintendent of the large (22,500 kids), poor (90% free lunch) Kansas City district. She has thoughtful priorities, is committed to innovation, and wants to reverse the perception among teachers that "the district won't let them do it." But having to cut $55 million from a budget of $355 million makes it awfully hard for even our best superintendents to improve learning. As an experienced businessperson, I can assure state leaders that the best path to business growth comes from high-quality schools that produce graduates ready for the workforce and that attract businesses and families to the state.

Milwaukee, Wisconsin—In visiting schools in the Milwaukee Public School (MPS) system, I was stunned to meet students who were commuting up to forty-five minutes each day, each way, to attend school. Worse, their commute keeps them from participating in after-school programs—so they miss the best part of their school day. For context, we need to go back to 1990, when Wisconsin enacted legislation providing families with vouchers to cover the costs of private school for their child. Seven years later, they followed with open enrollment legislation letting families choose any public school for their child.

This choice model is a key policy plank for Wisconsin's governor Scott Walker, for our nation's business-driven reformers, and for current secretary of education, Betsy DeVos. Apply free-market principles to fixing our schools. Given choice, families will pull their kids out of "dropout factories," driving these schools out of business. Better schools will thrive as they attract more students and resources. An unstated assumption is that preferred schools will generally be non-unionized charters, so choice will improve education as it weakens teachers' unions. Voilà.

But as I saw in Milwaukee, it's not that simple. Many families choose a school not because they think it's better but because it's far away. If their child spends more time on a bus each day, the parent can work longer hours without worrying about childcare. A long-time Milwaukee education leader explained, "Tens of thousands of kids are shuttling all over the city to attend a bad remote school instead of a bad local school. Our Wisconsin state motto is 'Forward,' but in education it's been nothing but 'backward' since 1990." Policies have consequences. The money Milwaukee spends supporting choice could be directed to incorporate PEAK learning in schools, training teachers, and feeding schoolchildren. If choice in Milwaukee is bringing about higher-quality classrooms or racial integration, I saw no sign of it.

I was in Milwaukee for their superb film festival, where *MLTS* drew a big crowd at the Downtown Oriental Theater. Always great when the festival's education documentary expert says to the audience, "The best film ever done on education reform." At one point, I got a ride from a festival volunteer who taught for years in the MPS system. Not knowing my views, he offered these suggestions for improving education: "Give teachers more respect, training, and professional development. Have kids learn more by doing instead of memorizing." After the screening, about a hundred people stayed to discuss education for three hours on a Sunday afternoon when a Green Bay Packers game was televised. No shortage of energy among these younger, diverse parents. In contrast, I met later with fifteen community leaders who had worked for years on Milwaukee education. I challenged them to brainstorm about ways to make Milwaukee's schools better than Finland's in ten years. They concluded, "It can't be done." This older generation seemed fatigued from years of unproductive effort tied to policies that sound great but haven't moved the needle in our schools.

We're too confident that parents make informed decisions about school. Most adults judge a school by its cover—facilities, test scores, the look of its people, or in some cases religious affiliation. Based on false impressions, families make mistakes. They pay exorbitant private school tuition, overpay for a house in a community with high test scores, or send their child across the city. When it comes to these "choice" policies, choice almost always stops at the school's front door. Once inside, the all-out push for higher test scores robs students and teachers of any agency. We're fooling ourselves with education "choice" that lets families choose among different obsolete schools.

I'm no fan of tenure—with K–12 schools, colleges, government, or anywhere, really. As I travel, though, the teachers I meet are passionate and dedicated. Put an excellent leader in a school and its teaching force soon follows—whether the school is private, public, or charter. The inverse is just as true. Yet for two decades, our education debate about tenure, charter, and vouchers has drawn our attention from the first-order issue of reimagining school.

_____   \\|//   _____

Nashville, Tennessee—Kevin Huffman served as Tennessee's commissioner of education from 2011 to 2015. He related, "While I was in college, I would have laughed at the thought of a career in education." But during his senior year at Swarthmore, he interviewed with TFA and took a position in Houston in the early 1990s, placing him right in the middle of the "no excuses" movement sparked by the Houston-based founders of the KIPP and YES Prep charter school networks. After his TFA stint, he went to law school, then back to TFA for a decade-long run with increasing main-office responsibilities as the organization scaled from $10 million to $200 million in annual budget. Along the way, he met and subsequently married Michelle Rhee, perhaps the country's most visible "no excuses" figure.

In 2011, Tennessee's newly elected governor recruited Huffman to be his education commissioner, just as the state was getting RTTP money to implement tough accountability measures. Fresh on the job, Huffman architected what he called "a massive overhaul"— adding charter schools, tying 35% of teacher compensation to test scores, and implementing differential compensation based on performance and roles (e.g., more pay for producing better test scores and more for teaching subjects like science and math). He pushed schools to excel in subjects key to the Tennessee Comprehensive Assessment Program, including Algebra II and Chemistry. He tied his agenda to Common Core. And, in 2013, Tennessee posted gains on their NAEP tests, often called the nation's report card. Yet despite this, Huffman explained, "People got pissed at a lot of the changes. The left was upset about charter, choice, and accountability, while the right was upset about Common Core. I saw populism here that we're now seeing in the [2016] presidential election."

He explained that Tennessee is a diverse, rural state. "People don't talk about solutions for rural," he noted, adding, "one-third of America lives in a world ignored by people making decisions." He viewed their Future Farmers of America programs as "moderately well run" but feels many CTE courses fall short. "When you drill down, it's Mickey Mouse.'" He laughed about a class he observed where students pretended to be police technicians drawing chalk outlines on the floor. "When do we get to the learning? There's not a lot there." He added, "There's a lot of bad math masquerading as applied CTE math." But Huffman was thoughtful and open to an expanded role: "The pivot to better CTE is incredibly difficult. But kids want it and could benefit from it."

Huffman's a big believer in standards. Without them, "people pretend that kids learn when they don't. Prior to 2010, 90% of Tennessee kids were 'proficient,' but our state was at or near the bottom. These people were good people, cared about kids, and want the best for Tennessee students. It's painful to accept that the work you're doing is wrong by the kid. People can and will make shit up to justify what is going on in school. Without a common standard, people just run loose, and we'll see enormous underperformance."

Huffman related that his most important personal discovery was the "enormous capacity for the existing workforce to learn and excel with adequate training. Go to any school in Tennessee, and you'll find at least two or three exceptional teachers. There are great people all over the place. But there are no systems to identify those who are exceptional, coach up others, provide everyone with effective professional development. A lot of people can step up and do great work if they get training and support." He added,

"I didn't do enough to elevate the best and give them the freedom to run. I would have given our better teachers more open runway."

Over coffee, Huffman seemed reflective about his time as Tennessee's commissioner, noting, "I continue to grapple with how difficult it is to build public appetite for change in education. It's easy to blame the political process, unions, policymakers. At the grassroots level, it's hard to get parents and teachers to seek change. The people most likely to embrace change are those most screwed over by the system." His final words were, "Many people were glad to see me go." And, in fact, he left amid controversy and calls for his resignation.

Huffman struck me as a good man, but here's my take. He took on the goal he believed he was given—increase test scores—and broke glass trying to do it. It seemed to work, for a while. Their 2013 NAEP score gains were touted as reformist triumph, but they were just a modest 2% bump that flattened in 2015 at a ho-hum level. Was it worth the animosity and polarization? Huffman, in many ways, represents the reform movement. Fighting to eke out test-score gains is education's equivalent of trying to win wars in Vietnam or Iraq. You can be a hard-charging general, but you won't succeed if you're leading a flawed mission that troops on the ground don't believe in.

Like many "do things better" educators, Huffman is an alum of TFA, an organization that deserves credit for attracting top college graduates to education. I met many on this trip. Most told me that they got a lot out of their TFA experience but weren't sure their students did. Their five weeks of training were completely inadequate for taking on challenging classrooms. I see a bigger issue with the TFA model. They recruit people who excelled in conventional school and want the same for their students. I saw this unquestioned commitment to academic hoop-jumping in most schools, districts, and states led by TFA alumni. One last telling anecdote. At a breakfast with a few education leaders, I commented, "We could do so much more with CTE in our schools." Sitting next to me, a very, very senior TFA executive asked, "What's CTE?"

Tallahassee, Florida—The meeting was short. I met with the chief of staff to Florida governor Rick Scott, who advises him, and previously Jeb Bush, on education. Her staff rescheduled a few times, but she met me at 2:45 p.m. in her office in the Florida State Capitol. Let's refer to her as KM. I introduced myself and began explaining what I was doing. I tend to talk fast but after a couple of minutes, KM stopped me. "Look. I know everything I need to know about education. You don't need to tell me anything. What can I explain to you?"

> Me: I believe that the more test-driven a school is, the more it puts kids at risk in a world of innovation.
>
> KM: You're making this too complicated. Educating children is like fixing a car. You take a car to the garage and pay them to fix it. We pay our schools $7,000 per student and expect them to be educated.
>
> Me: How do you know they're learning anything?
>
> KM: That's why we have standardized tests.

When I started to respond, KM stood up and informed me, "Look. I'm important to the governor. Thank you for your time." And left. In a year with a thousand meetings, this was the worst.

To illustrate how the Florida legislature and executive branch think about education, consider this. In 2015, Governor Scott signed into law a bill that included Florida's Best and Brightest Teacher Scholarship Program. A Florida public school teacher rated as "highly effective," or any first-year teacher irrespective of evaluations, is eligible for a $10,000 bonus. But in order to receive this $10,000, the teacher needs to have scored in the top 20% on *his or her* SAT or ACT test. Not the scores of the students, but the teacher's own test scores! We're talking about teachers who might have taken their SATs decades ago. To receive the bonus, teachers have to dig up old scores and submit them to the Florida Department of Education. An amazing social studies teacher transforming students' lives won't get this bonus if his or her standardized test scores fall below the top 20% threshold. A fumbling first-year teacher with high test scores will. So teachers have a financial incentive to take test-prep courses, drill, and retake the SAT/ACT until they break into the top 20%. Last year, the Florida state government set aside $44 million to fund this bonus program, money that could have gone to better teacher training, student programs, and basic nutrition for their low-income students.

A number of people I met this year would tell me, often in a whisper, that our schools of education aren't attracting the best students. I'd respond, "How do you know?" They'd say, "Well, the average test scores for education majors are low." To which I'd say, "When you think of outstanding teachers you had, what were their strengths?" People cite empathy, bringing a subject to life, being a great role model, providing helpful feedback, asking thought-provoking questions, making learning fun, helping them believe in their potential. To date, no one has said, "High standardized test scores."

If state legislators think test scores are so important, they should release their own. If we want the Best and Brightest teaching our children, we shouldn't settle for less in the Florida State House. Dollars to donuts, these officials would never publish their scores. They'd explain that being a state legislator is that one position in life where other competencies are more important. But they have no qualms about pushing a test-prep agenda on their students and teachers.

JoAnne McCall heads the Florida Education Association teachers' union. When it comes to teachers' unions, beware of sweeping statements. I often hear people, particularly businesspeople, say, "We'll never fix our schools until we get rid of teachers' unions and tenure." My former self leaned toward that view a decade ago. For sure, some unions take bureaucratic, even nonsensical, positions that don't serve the interests of our kids. But in my travels, the teachers I meet are dedicated, whether or not they hold a union card. When any school has the right principal, its teaching force hits its stride. I've found teachers' unions generally quite supportive of change that makes sense. We need to temper criticism of teachers and their unions with a reality check on what we're doing to the profession. Teachers are underpaid, micromanaged, and held accountable to measures they don't believe in, nor should they. We're driving out many and demoralizing most. The pipeline of new teachers is drying up in most states. Despite it all, they remain committed to our children.

For families in states like Florida, I feel your pain. Your children can't fight dumb policies, but you can. If you're in a test-and-measure state, petition high-ranking state officials and legislators to release their standardized test scores. Insist that they take the end-of-course assessments required of all high school students and publish their scores. One last offer to any state with school policies mired in test/measure/accountability. If you can get policymakers to agree to debate the future of your schools, I'll be there and fund its broadcast to all state residents.

Everything has a context. McCall's context is the state of Florida, whose past governor Jeb Bush often invoked this quote about education: "If you can't count it, it doesn't matter." Bush and his fellow data hawks are living in the past. In the twenty-first century, they should quote noted author Brené Brown: "When it comes to education, if you can measure it, it probably doesn't matter." Instead of viewing teachers as the enemy, they might want to listen to Andrew Carnegie, a philanthropist who re-shaped learning across America: "Teamwork is the ability to work together toward a common vision. It is the fuel that allows common people to attain uncommon results."

Doing Better Things

Our country does have education leaders who are transforming schools at scale. This sounds simple enough, but it's been the bugaboo of U.S. education for decades. We've struggled to scale our successes, largely due to confusion about what to scale. We latch onto new curriculum or testing regimens or accountability measures, which we then roll out with a command-and-control model. Yet another round of teaching all students standardized material, in standardized ways, to a new battery of standardized tests. After decades of trying, about all we've managed to scale is failure.

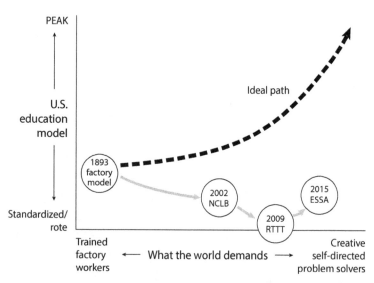

FIGURE 9.1. The Misdirected Path of U.S. Education Policy.

We're about to see what happens when leaders focus on scale at the meta-level. Rather than pushing detailed prescriptions into classrooms, they scale the conditions that empower their teachers and students to create compelling learning experiences. These leaders trust their teachers, treating them as partners. There's genuine collaboration in designing authentic assessments. Transformational leaders pave the way so that students, teachers, and principals can "do better things." They know what school could be, and how to get there.

America's greatness comes from its creativity, drive, and pioneering spirit. We do the most amazing things in the arts and sciences, in business and social change. Our form of government affords people the latitude to pursue their passions, to forge their path, to flourish. During the Cold War, we saw the power of these organizing principles when the United States faced off against the centrally planned USSR. History leaves no doubt about which model brings out the best in its population. But in the realm of education, our policies come right from the Soviet playbook. Now, we'll meet leaders drawing on principles that undergird our country's strength.

Providence, Rhode Island—Ted and Nancy Sizer are giants in education. Founders of the Providence-based Coalition of Essential Schools in 1984, they offer an inspiring view of what our schools, teachers, and students can do. They changed the lives of many, and I ran into Sizer protégés everywhere I traveled. Ted, who passed away in 2009, and Nancy Sizer have dedicated their lives to showing American schools a path forward.

Ted Sizer's most famous work is *Horace's Compromise*, published in 1984 shortly after the *A Nation at Risk* report. It centers on a mythical high school teacher, Horace Smith, facing compromises in teaching high school English. One compromise is how he allocates his time to preparing, teaching, grading, and one-on-one meetings. On a different level, Horace feels a sense of compromise between inspiring students and functioning in a system that pulls against the aspirational.

Horace lives in an education world where honors students "dodge the hard problems, the hard courses to keep their averages up," conning colleges in the process. Where most students have been made "docile, compliant, and without initiative" by schools that give "few rewards for being inquisitive," students "see the diploma as their high school goal, the passport to the next stage of life," and earn it through seat time. Far better, Sizer argues, for competency-based standards—"Place the emphasis on ends, on exhibited mastery." The following passage was particularly striking, given it was written over three decades ago:

> We live today, crowded together, in a culture overloaded with information, surfeited with data and opinions and experiences that we pump up with the buttons on our TV sets, home computers, telephones, and word processors. The world around us, for good or ill, is a more insistent, rich, and effective provider of information than was our grandparents'. Education's job today is less in purveying information than in helping people to use it—that is, to exercise their minds."[14]

In many important ways, the Sizers were ahead of their time, laying out an inspiring agenda. I felt honored after getting this out-of-the-blue note from Nancy Sizer after she had seen *MLTS* at the Harvard Graduate School of Education (HGSE):

> The whole walk back from HGSE, I had tears in my eyes wishing that he [Ted] could have seen your work. It was not only the right message: we in the Coalition of Essential Schools consider High Tech High to be our beloved "child," and Ted

was the one who introduced the word "exhibition" into its modern usage as the kind of assessment which makes sense for students. But also as a piece of art, it was very moving.

_____ \\|// _____

Occasionally, someone will ask if ideas like learning by doing, or conditions that empower, are just another education fad, like the latest round of new math. But these important ideas date back. To Ted Sizer, who said, "Inspiration, hunger: these are the qualities that drive good schools. The best we education planners can do is to create the most likely conditions for them to flourish, and then get out of the way." To John Dewey, who said, "Give the pupils something to do, not something to learn; and the doing is of such a nature as to demand thinking; learning naturally results." To the long sweep of civilization, where great artists, scientists, and civic leaders learned through apprenticeships at the hands of masters.

Historians can debate whether the United States would have been better-off in 1893 following Dewey's views instead of the Committee of Ten's effective approach. And when the Sizers launched the Coalition of Essential Schools, graduates of conventional schools weren't running headlong into roadblocks. But today's world is exacting, even ruthless. In the last century, the views of these education visionaries were important. In this century, they are indispensable.

_____ \\|// _____

Olympia, Washington—Randy Dorn served two terms as Washington State's superintendent of public instruction. His career spans teaching elementary and middle school, serving as a principal, heading the Public School Employees organization, serving in the state legislature, and six years as a motivational speaker (easy to believe). He's fought to reduce the role of standardized testing in schools, to increase school funding, and to expand preschool options for the poor. He's worked productively with businesses to help students gain skills they can apply to their world. He's a big believer in internships and apprenticeships, for both students and teachers. He notes the benefits of having math teachers meet engineers at local companies (e.g., Boeing, Microsoft) to observe math in the workplace.

Dorn rat-a-tats you with success stories about schools in his state—no two alike. Aviation High School, Delta High School, School of the Arts in Tacoma, and many more. He elaborated on Tacoma's Science and Math Institute (SAMI), located next to the Point Defiance Zoo and Aquarium. "Do you know that 62% of Tacoma kids have never been to the zoo? Show me a kid that isn't interested in a class on primates." The common denominator is kids wanting to learn. "Look what we do to our kids. If you're a low-performing student, we pull you out of the classes you enjoy and make you do more rote math. If you're still not doing well, summer school. Why?"

Dorn underscores one of education's biggest problems: "Our kids don't know why they're being educated other than to go to college." The role of intrinsic motivation has been completely lost in our schools. Dorn noted the opening scene of MLTS where a fourth-grader is in tears during her parent-teacher conference while adults talk about her. One of Dorn's schools moved to student-led conferences and were shocked to see 98% of parents attending, up from 25% the prior year. He's learned that even kindergartners can effectively lead a parent-teacher-student conference and wonders why any parent-teacher conferences would exclude the student. One of Dorn's schools is Garfield High School, the epicenter of the opt-out movement. In my visit there, I asked several students why they had boycotted standardized tests. Most responded, "My parents told me to." That's not helping. We should ask students to research the issues around testing and make their own decisions about whether to participate.

Dorn's experience is that you can change an elementary school in twelve months, since K–6 teachers teach kids. It's much harder to change a high school, since high school teachers teach subjects. A reporter recently asked him, "Why are charter schools more innovative than public schools?" His response: "I don't know that they are. There's nothing a charter school can do that is prohibited from a public school." But he notes that many public school administrators cite regulations that keep them from innovating. "I have the power to grant waivers, and will. But I haven't gotten a single request."

On the topic of data, one Washington state district regularly asks its students, teachers, principals, and central office administrators these questions:

1. Do you feel safe at school?
2. Is there someone senior to you that you can talk to when you have a concern?
3. Do you have pride in your school?
4. Would you recommend your school to a friend at a different school?
5. Is the work you are assigned at school meaningful?
6. Do you look forward to coming to school each day?

Our education system spends billions of dollars collecting data precisely measuring student progress on material they'll probably never use. Few schools gather data on important questions like these, something they can do for free with SurveyMonkey.

A big impediment to innovation comes when school leaders assume change isn't possible. The Nellie Mae Foundation commissioned a study to determine what prevents principals from making changes. Of blocking factors cited by principals, some 69% don't exist.[15] Schools with the right leadership can innovate, irrespective of state and federal requirements. Engaged and motivated students do just fine on mandated tests, despite no test prep. College place-ments won't suffer when high school students are doing compel-ling work. While it might seem daunting to transform a school's culture and classrooms, it all starts with a shift in mind-set.

— — — — —   ⟍⎮╱   — — — — —

Newark, New Jersey—Newark's East Side High School (ESHS) is a comprehensive public high school with 1,300 students. It's a melting pot of ethnicities, mostly kids of color and lots of recent immigrants. One thing these students have in common: poverty. Dr. Mario Santos, the school's principal, graduated from ESHS in 1995, never imagining he'd return. After starting his career as an elementary school teacher, he got his PhD with plans to move into administration. As he was finishing his doctorate, he bumped into an ESHS student. When Santos asked how school was going, the student "looked at me with this blank stare and said, 'It's all right but people don't really care. I haven't seen my math teacher in months.' " Santos was shaken. As fate would have it, he got an offer that week to be East Side's principal. "I said to myself, 'I'm going to make that school a great school.' " Twelve years later, Santos hasn't looked back.

Santos came into a tough situation. In 2006, some 70% of the students were failing some classes, and just 90 out of 2,000 were on the honor roll. Today, failure rates have been slashed, and 700 are on the honor roll. With justifiable pride, Santos notes, "I now have students starting college as juniors with an associate's degree. We're providing opportunities for kids to believe in themselves." If you go by test data, ESHS lags peers in wealthy enclaves like Far Hills or Upper Saddle River. But Santos's kids aren't spending time outside of school with tutors or squash coaches. "Our kids are deal-ing with crime, murder, gangs."

East Side's challenges start before the morning's first bell. "I don't want one child hungry. We feed all kids every morning during instructional time in the classroom. We have 80 classrooms, 2,000 kids. It's major logistics entirely run by the kids. It's been hugely successful." Santos makes the program available to all kids. "You can't just walk into a classroom and ask a kid if he had breakfast. He's not going to tell you he doesn't have food in the house." The stress these kids face is real and deep—a drug-addicted sibling, an incarcerated parent, finding the next meal, or being evicted from miserable housing. Santos brought in the Youth Empowerment Seminars program to "teach breathing techniques, yoga, and meditation. My teachers go through it, too. Some said it was the best professional development they've had in fifteen years. It's teaching people how to calm down, stay focused, get grounded."

Most of Santos's kids have gotten years of test-score feedback about their academic inadequacies. "We're looking at how we can reengage these kids. Get away from the drilling and killing of academics. Obviously, academics are important, but to what extent? We're not all going to be scientists or mathematicians. There are lots of other pathways, other skills. The economy calls for soft skills, language skills, creativity, teamwork." Santos adds, "The problem with education's traditional model is that school is boring. It's damn boring. I'm not saying we need a party every day, but we need to engage kids in creative thinking, to connect their learning to the real world." Santos is a proponent of internships. "A student works at the aquarium once a week and brings back a new outlook on school. When you get kids engaged in meaningful, hard work, you see kids lighting the fire." Santos observes, "Can you get a kid to stay up till 2 a.m. and on weekends doing math homework? No. Where's the passion in a Pearson textbook? It's not relevant. But if you get a kid to build a house or make a documentary, school is a different experience. That's more and more what we want to do."

Santos is part educator and part entrepreneur. His daily reality is, "Do I buy the extra copiers or put the money into programs that work?" He's masterful at bringing in outside partners to help transform the lives of his kids, including two impressive nonprofits. Big Picture Learning helps kids in low socioeconomic circumstances access internships, mentors, advisors, and meaningful real-world projects. The Future Project places a charismatic "Dream Director" in partner schools to help students pursue their aspirations for improving their community and their lives. Santos found funding for a cutting-edge Future Shop equipped with a 3D Printer, a sewing machine, a vinyl cutter, a 42" plotter, a heat press, a silk-screen press, laptops, CAD software, and photography equipment. The initiative's director, Luisa Reyes, notes:

> Students using the space learn practical skills that stoke their curiosity—and equip them to succeed in college and in today's innovation economy. Students learn 3D modeling, digital design, design thinking, audio/visual production, and experimentation (tinkering). They're developing critical mind-sets and twenty-first-century skills—creativity, open-mindedness, self-awareness, and collaboration. It's outstanding to see the transformation in these students.

Steadily and cost-effectively, Mario Santos is showing the world how to transform a failing inner-city public school. "Imagine how much lost potential is out there. Our system shuts many kids out because they don't do well on standardized tests. Einstein was assessed as an idiot, and he was one of the most intelligent human beings to walk this planet. If we can create systems that tap into the unique creative potential of each human being, the future is limitless." He concluded, "We are the change agents. We are in the system, yes, but we have to continue to change it."

Santos filled me in on Oscar, "one of those at-risk kids. His dad's in prison, his brother is a drug dealer. It's not easy." Oscar hoped to attend ESHS at a time when there weren't any open spots. Santos recalls, "I'm walking into school and Oscar's sitting on a milk crate at 7:45 a.m. He'd been there since 6 a.m. This kid was fighting for his

education, so I decided to do whatever I could to get him here."
At the end of a session with ESHS students, Oscar approached me
with some thoughtful questions and observations. His closing comment stopped me in my tracks: "We read in history class about how
adults in our country worked together long ago to put someone
on the moon. Do you think adults can work together to make our
schools great?" I was close to speechless, barely managing, "I sure
hope so, Oscar."

As fate would have it, I was in Newark when Dale Russakoff was
in town for a press conference about her book *The Prize: Who's in
Charge of America's Schools?* She chronicles a philanthropic initiative seeking to improve education in Newark that involved Cory
Booker, Chris Christie, and Mark Zuckerberg. In total, some $200 mil-
lion was spent to create a bold new paradigm for education reform.
Most would agree that, put charitably, this could have gone better.
Of the $200 million, only a trickle made its way to the schools; for
example, ESHS got a whopping $5,000. High-paid consultants set the
agenda, largely bypassing input from Newark's students, teachers,
and families. They aspired to a new paradigm without addressing
the core issue of a century-old education model.

Imagine if Zuckerberg, a college dropout and remarkable entrepreneur, had said to Booker and Christie, "Guys, today's graduates
need to be creative, determined problem solvers. Let's help kids in
all Newark schools build these competencies. Let's work with Newark's principals, teachers, and students to set priorities and bring
cultures of innovation to their schools. Provide resources that engage kids—makerspaces, creative arts studios, robotics, theater,
design thinking. Get local organizations to provide mentors, internships, apprenticeships, equipment, and training. Rally the community around an aspirational view of what Newark's schools can
be. If we take this approach, I'm in." But to move a community's
schools ahead, we need to start with unsung heroes like Mario Santos. In words that could be Zuckerberg's, Santos said, "If it's not

working, then I'm going to do it differently. You gotta be a little bit crazy in this world, otherwise you get caught up going through motions that just don't make sense."

Boise, Idaho—Almost every community has a philanthropist or good-sized foundation doing great education work. In Idaho, the dream benefactor is the J. A. and Kathryn Albertson Family Foundation. The Albertsons made their fortune through their grocery store chain and are now giving back to their home state. Their mission: "Limitless Learning for All Idahoans." In 2015, the Albertson Family Foundation brought MLTS to forty-four communities in Idaho, so I was thrilled to be invited to Boise to deliver a keynote to a meeting convened by One Stone, one of their grantees.

With the tagline "Design for Good," One Stone is about innovation, design thinking, and social entrepreneurship. Students work with local organizations to identify problems and create tech-leveraged solutions. For example, One Stone has a student-run design/marketing agency providing pro bono expertise to local organizations. Students make their community better while learning skills that matter. Two birds with one stone. Starting with just eight students in 2008, One Stone has grown to two hundred students across Idaho. It's currently an after-school initiative, so students attend a conventional high school during the day. A One Stone student shared this perspective:

> I've taken lots of AP classes, and their nature is teaching to that test and covering extensive content on a schedule. Nothing mastery or inquiry based. That model doesn't prepare you for the world, just basic coverage of content. Inquiry-based learning allows you to wrap your mind around a subject rather than around a text. Become a more inquisitive learner. My favorite experience in school was on the debate team, because I got to learn what's going on in the world, about em-

pathy, current events. Nowhere else in my high school experience do I get that.

Unlike typical education conferences, the One Stone event was planned and carried out entirely by students. Refreshing. These students had deep insight into education and were articulate on the urgency for reimagining school. The event's centerpiece was a student-led Twenty-Four-Hour Think Challenge. The group started with amorphous ideas and distilled them into a vision for a new school in Boise. No grade levels or grades, just digital portfolios reflecting authentic accomplishment. Adults serve as coaches, not teachers. Student internships connect their learning to the real world and help them create careers. The physical space is open and collaborative, with a state-of-the-art makerspace. Longer term, they plan to scale this microschool across their state, changing Idaho's education landscape. PEAK principles, driven by students, supported by a thoughtful foundation, creating an initiative that can effect change at scale.

While our mega-foundations write the big checks, local foundations and philanthropists do the best work in education. They take risks and respond quickly to proposals. They care deeply about their community and spend considerable time in the field observing the impact of their grants. In contrast, program officers with large foundations have limited time for field visits and need data for their internal reports. It's a rare mega-foundation that will cut a small check to fund a risky new initiative, particularly one whose ultimate impact might be hard to measure.

From 1883 through 1925, Andrew Carnegie personally funded 1,689 libraries across America. He didn't insist that libraries administer multiple-choice tests to all book borrowers to produce data about impact. He didn't demand weekly reports on the number of books borrowed, returned, or lost. He didn't weigh in on how to organize or compensate the adults staffing the libraries. He just did something bold that brought joyful education to millions.

— — — — —   \\ | / /   — — — — —

Charlottesville, Virginia—A public school district in central Virginia is quietly emerging as a national leader in transforming schools at scale. Pam Moran, superintendent of the Albemarle County Public Schools (ACPS) District, dizzies you with compelling sound bites. "Many of our students don't need remediation. They need a mission." "When kids feel like a school is a great place to be, they learn." "Making things is what we're about."

Moran describes how her first day as a teacher shaped her core education values. Wanting to start things with a bang, this aspiring young science teacher brought a canvas bag to her very first class. She asked her students to guess what was in the bag, then pulled out a long snake. Seconds after assuring her kids that the snake was harmless, it bit her arm and blood gushed out. With her class in chaos, the principal happened to drop by. She was called into his office later that day, certain she'd be fired. Instead he said, "The way you'll become a great teacher is by trying bold things. Good for you."

I first heard about Pam in the context of controversy. John Hunter is an exceptional fourth-grade teacher who ventures outside the lines. He invented a game called World Peace—a sort of three-dimensional Risk on steroids—that immerses students into global diplomacy, with electrifying impact. But his principal (at a school in the abutting district) took issue with straying from the text. When Hunter left, Moran pounced. Days later he was teaching at an elementary school in her district. Hunter's work inspired the documentary *World Peace and Other Fourth Grade Achievements*. His class has been hosted at the Pentagon to provide guidance about training our next generation of global strategists.

When Moran brought *MLTS* to her district, Albemarle High School's community watched it and lightbulbs went on. Their principal, Jay Thomas, wanted to transform learning in his school and, with Moran's support, encouraged his team to brainstorm. Had Moran and Thomas dictated changes, they'd have been bogged down in complaints for years. Instead, they empowered teachers and students to create their own program. Not all students and teachers but those passionate about reimagining learning. Four faculty members and sixty-five entering freshmen took the leap. Teachers put in long hours over the summer, and when school opened in August, some 20% of the entering class entered a new world of learning. Students work in teams on projects, schedules are completely restructured, and bells are ignored. They draw on resources like the school's music studio, leveraging student passion for composing and playing music to spark learning in adjacent areas—the math and history of music, the physics of acoustics, and the power of language. Small sparks lead to bonfires of learning, for a student and for a school.

Moran's approach reflects something fundamental about what motivates people to excel. When people are ordered to do something they don't believe in, they go through the motions. When they take ownership of their goal, they blow you away. Agency and purpose. ACPS empowered teachers and students to create a school-within-a-school. After a successful first year, the program scaled the following year to 150 students and eleven teachers. With support from Moran, ACPS's Monticello High School created its own distinctive school-within-a-school initiative. This is how innovation works—decentralized, bottom-up, driven by those who create and own the work.

Eminence, Kentucky—In a poor region of a poor state, Kentucky's Buddy Berry leads the Eminence Independent school district. Berry is the fourth generation in his family to be educated in Eminence schools. It's safe to say his ancestors' school looked nothing like Eminence today. Berry explains,

> Eminence innovated from a place of hope and desperation. Our school was faced with struggling test scores, declining enrollment, and a lack of identity. It was from a place of desperation that we decided to create what we considered would be the school of our dreams, the Disney World of Schools. We knew that students needed more from their learning experiences than simply scoring well on an exam and so we tried to create the school of the future . . . today.

With support from his school board and parent community, Berry thought big. He introduced his Framework of Innovation for Re-Inventing Education (FIRE). Kentucky House Bill 37, enacted in 2012, allows up to ten of Kentucky's 173 school districts to be "innovation districts," freed from many regulations and statutory provisions. Eminence jumped at this opportunity. Eminence schools feature student-driven, teacher-guided learning, with lots of time for exploration. Berry notes that student agency isn't just listening to students complain: it's deeply trusting them to own their learning and to identify and solve problems in their school and community.

Initially, innovation resulted in lower test scores, something Berry cautioned his community to expect. Over time, scores have increased both in overall levels and in the rate of improvement. While his kindergartners continue to score poorly, his high school kids score in Kentucky's top 5%—even though Eminence expressly doesn't teach to the test. Students there enthusiastically describe ambitious projects and answer questions with precision and confidence. All this, in a poor rural public school district in the middle of nowhere. A district that now has families driving fifty miles each way each day so their kids can attend a school on FIRE.

In traveling around Kentucky, people kept referring with admiration to Kara. I felt guilty not remembering her. When I first meet someone, my brain freezes up precisely when they say their name. Given how frequently Kara's name came up, I assumed she helped organize my visit and was influential in Kentucky education circles. But I couldn't connect a face with that name. During my visit, Justin Bathon, a respected University of Kentucky professor, walked me through his state's education history. Kentucky's school system in the 1980s was forty-ninth or fiftieth on every metric. Education got a kick in the pants from a 1989 court case, when school superintendents sued the state on the grounds that Kentucky education was inadequate. In *Rose v. Council for Better Education*, their Supreme Court ruled in favor of the superintendents, declaring without qualification that "the common school system in Kentucky is constitutionally deficient." The General Assembly was ordered to get things on track by the opening of the next school year. They swiftly enacted the Kentucky Education Reform Act (KERA). Ah, KERA. Not Kara. Mystery solved.

KERA transformed education in Kentucky, in part by increasing funding levels by over a billion dollars. But it did much more. It laid out well-conceived goals for educating Kentucky's children. It introduced accountability into schools in ways that were diagnostic and constructive, not punitive. It raised teaching standards and ended the practice of nepotistic hires plaguing rural schools. It changed the funding formula to ensure more equity across districts. It brought people together with a shared goal. Bathon's bottom line: "KERA put Kentucky on the education map." By the early 2000s, Kentucky had moved into the second and even first quartile on traditional education metrics. This progress was astounding, particularly in a state short on natural resources and booming businesses. In Bathon's words, "The great lesson with Kentucky is that it is possible to take great leaps forward." He added, "The story of Kentucky is not about massive superstar charter schools but of multiple core public schools trying to improve. It was the system itself trying to get better. And that's powerful." And with modest support, leaders like Buddy Berry can work miracles in the most unlikely of places.

Montpelier, Vermont—Vermont inherited the compelling philosophy of native son John Dewey. Born there in 1859, Dewey made profound contributions to philosophy, psychology, government, and education, with a focus on education's role in democracy and civil society. He argued that education is social and that students should be empowered to own their learning. Education shouldn't be about acquiring narrow content or specific skills, but helping students reach their full potential, and directing this potential to the greater good. Dewey cautioned that an uneducated population poses a threat to our democracy, words all the more resonant during a travel year coinciding with the 2016 presidential election.

If Dewey could pick someone to lead Vermont's public school system, he'd select Rebecca Holcombe, the state's secretary of education. She grew up with parents who worked for the United Nations, attended schools in Afghanistan and Pakistan, and earned her PhD in education from Harvard. Early in her career, she taught and then became principal of the Fairlee public high school, earning a reputation for vision and innovation. Over time, she's taken on increasing responsibilities, becoming influential nationally. She doesn't parrot back tired platitudes. She challenges the "college for all" mantra, arguing instead that all kids need to be "innovation ready" for a dynamic world full of ambiguity. She pushed for Vermont's Act 77, which empowers all Vermont students to define their personal pathway to graduation and advance on the basis of demonstrated proficiency, not seat time.

Vermont has one of the nation's best overall public education systems. But NCLB criteria rated every single public school there as *low-performing*. Mind you, these same schools consistently rank among the world's leaders on Program for International Student Assessment (PISA) and NAEP tests. This seeming indictment actually freed them to implement bold initiatives. However, as one of five states that didn't comply with Arne Duncan's RTTT accountability measures, Vermont had to inform every public-school family that their child was attending a failing school. Holcombe's letter included this telling paragraph:

> This policy does not serve the interest of Vermont schools, nor does it advance our economic or social well-being. Further, it takes our focus away from other measures that give us more meaningful and useful data on school effectiveness.

A stone's throw from Holcombe's office is U-32, a name suggestive of a rock group or submarine. But U-32 is a school in Montpelier, the capital of a state whose school districts are called "supervisory unions," or U's. Walking around this grade 7–12 school, you sense something different. About one-third of their students participate in their "community-based learning" program with credit awarded for meaningful internships. Their Branching Out program lets any high school student pick a topic of interest, find a mentor, and spend the equivalent of a yearlong course on something they're interested in, for credit. Students can do this multiple times during their high school years.

A few years ago, U-32 initiated Pilot, a program allowing students to create their *entire* learning program for a year. I met with several students who credited Pilot with reviving their interest in learning, in some cases keeping them in school. Back to John Dewey: give students agency and they'll do amazing things. One artistic young woman hated regular school but is now making progress with her art, learning graphic and website design, and will graduate with strong career prospects. Another self-proclaimed "gun nut" said he was ready to drop out to enlist in the military when he enrolled in Pilot. He related that while he read no books the prior year, this year he's "devouring books, including antiwar books that help me understand both perspectives." He spoke knowledgeably about the chemistry and physics of various types of weaponry. After completing his high school degree, he'll decide whether to go on to college or directly into the armed services. In either event, he's on a path to make positive contributions to society. Left ignored and disaffected, who knows how this might have played out.

In the midst of great stories was something equivocal. A young woman nailed her grades as a freshman but felt she wasn't learning. She spent her sophomore year with Pilot, focusing on government, politics, and women's studies. As part of this experience, she had an internship with a lobbying firm, gaining insight into how Vermont's government functions. While passionate about Pilot, she'll be back in the mainstream program as a junior, explaining that she feels pressure to take AP courses for her college application.

Concord, New Hampshire—During an eight-year period under impressive leadership, New Hampshire became our nation's single best example of education transformation—thoughtful, systemic, empowering, and effective. America needs to pay attention to how they innovated, bringing PEAK principles to schools across the state.

Tom Raffio, the dynamic young CEO of New Hampshire Delta Dental, is an inspiring leader in New Hampshire's education renaissance. First appointed to the New Hampshire State School Board in 2007, Raffio assumed the role of chairman in 2011. Serving on a state board is an uncompensated labor of love. Raffio committed five full business days each month to school board issues, including monthly all-day board meetings—not easy for a full-time CEO.

The state school board doesn't control local school boards but does rule on appeals of local decisions. Monthly board meetings allocate about a half day to bureaucratic issues like arbitrating these appeals and a half day to what Raffio calls the "fun part"—hearing from teachers and students about best practices. Raffio travels extensively on behalf of New Hampshire's education system, setting a positive tone, explaining changes and innovations, and soliciting feedback. He works with state legislators to make sure their actions further the interests of students. Atypically, this state board oversees the state's community colleges and four-year colleges, as well as K–12. Raffio's role as chair of New Hampshire's Coalition for Business and Education helps him align interests. He collaborates with state colleges (University of New Hampshire, Keene State, and Franklin Pierce) on professional development strategies for the state's next generation of teachers. When asked about his state's highest education priority, Raffio responded without hesitation: "Student engagement."

Raffio is effusive in his praise for New Hampshire's "fantastic" commissioner of education, Ginny Barry, proud to be her "biggest cheerleader." Appointed by the governor, Barry assumed her leadership position in 2009. During her eight years as commissioner, she championed deep and important advances in her state's education system and established herself as a global education leader. Barry and her team have demonstrated the power of competency-based graduation requirements and performance-based assessments. New Hampshire's ten flagship PACE (Performance Assessment of Competency Education) districts now draw thousands of visitors annually from all over the country.

Dr. Brian Blake, recently named New Hampshire's Superintendent of the Year, and Ellen Hume-Howard, his curriculum director, explained how PACE works in their Sanborn Public School District. They've shifted to an entirely student-centered environment for all schools—elementary, middle, and high school. Students design their own schedules, often working in a classroom for hours at a time immersed in projects. Many courses are integrated across traditional subject boundaries. Even traditional classes look different—no students sitting passively in rows listening to a lecture. To move to the next level, students must demonstrate in-depth mastery of the material. Hume-Howard explains, "We work on a four-point scale, with an emphasis on descriptors rather than numbers. Kids see rubrics that highlight what should be expected. It's about what they produce." Students get grades and occasionally take standardized tests selectively for calibration. She elaborated, "Third grade is the year where you want to see if kids are at reading level, so that's when teachers use the English assessment. Fourth grade is a good time to test math skills, because scores at that age predict later success in math. It's not that teachers hate every test, we just need to embrace the right kinds of assessments and ensure our kids are doing things that are valuable to them." Currently, their early grade teachers use the Smarter Balanced assessment.

Blake explained that PACE goes beyond assessment. It's about trusting teachers to define accountability for themselves and their students. "We used PACE to lift expectations for everyone." Sanborn meets annually with New Hampshire's other PACE districts to cross-check their competency-based standards. In a recent session to ensure consistency, districts reviewed random samples of student work, along with the competency assessment each received. Across hundreds of samples, only a half dozen prompted debate. Teachers set their goals and help design a system of checks and balances. As I saw in my business career, people trusted to set their own goals push themselves and go to the ends of the earth to succeed.

As Sanborn began implementing changes, Blake estimated that some "75–80% of parents were in support, 10–15% were silent, and a small percentage thought we were ruining their kid's life. What we found was the high-achieving kids, the ones that had learned to play the game of school—memorizing and regurgitating facts but can't remember them two days later or apply what they have learned—they and their parents were the most resistant. Well, what they were worried about didn't happen. They are still playing the game, but now they play for competency."

Hume-Howard explained, "This isn't something the state is pushing down. Success is coming from the ground up, from the work our teachers do every day with our kids." She talked about how "NCLB took away teacher confidence. We spent a lot of the time in this district building our teachers up so that they feel like experts at this. In our system, teachers know that their judgment means something. Now we are seeing teachers flying. It's huge."

New Hampshire's leadership set the conditions enabling districts, schools, and classrooms to innovate. Sanborn's Hume-Howard credits the New Hampshire Department of Education and state legislators for "being supportive in listening to the field and getting out of the way. New Hampshire passed policies and legislation that gave us a leg up. For example, policy allows us to merge and integrate subject areas. It paved the way." Administrators like Blake and Hume-Howard thrive in environments where transformational leaders like Raffio and Barry offer support and direction.

We've just seen leaders effecting inspiring change in schools, at scale. While their approaches differ, each draws on an innovation change model that empowers their teachers and students. They're establishing conditions that let classrooms flourish. To understand their approaches, I spent considerable time observing them in action in all sorts of settings, with teachers, students, and parents. Here's what stood out.

For starters, these transformational leaders are effective communicators and stay on message about the importance of change. They energize constituencies in their community with a compelling vision of how they can best prepare students for a very different world. They deliver a compelling one-two punch—the urgency and the breathtaking possibility. Second, they articulate an aspirational goal for student outcomes, often in the context of essential skill sets and mind-sets. This profile provides teachers with high-level direction in crafting learning experiences. Third, they give teachers and principals permission to innovate—and repeat this message emphatically. They want their schools to embrace cultures of innovation. They trust teachers to take small steps leading to big change. Fourth, they empower teachers to design authentic accountability frameworks subject to checks and balances, something we saw in New Hampshire. Fifth, they know from experience that systemic change doesn't happen overnight. To effect deep transformation, they adopt the iterative principles of design thinking and at times rely on expert partners. Finally, they enlist their community in the aspirational goal of reimagining school, inviting them to participate through in-school visits, internships, equipment and funding, and moral support.

It takes courage and vision for a leader to adopt these principles. They give up control. They risk small failures in a "gotcha" world where social media can blow up the minuscule. They put their career on the line to do what they know is best for their students. They're helping us understand an innovation change model that creates the conditions for PEAK learning, at scale.

Vancouver, British Columbia—During a short detour to Vancouver, I met Mike Lombardi, chairman of the Vancouver School Board. Their progress underscores why the United States should pay close attention to education across the border. Canada has no federal Department of Education. Provinces allot the same budget dollars to educating each child—irrespective of local wealth. They've done away with standardized testing in their schools, focusing instead on critical skills, for which Lombardi credited Tony Wagner. Teachers have objectives for student learning and are trusted to help their students reach high-level goals. Their equivalent of Common Core standards consists of short descriptions of proficiency expectations for each grade and subject. Although they don't teach to the test, their PISA scores are exceptional. Colleges in British Columbia are highly rated, affordable, and don't require standardized tests for admission.

A breath of education fresh air, in a city barely beyond the U.S. border.

It Takes a Village

Change is nigh impossible when people dump on anything new. Many educators have learned how hard it is to break from tradition in the face of passive-aggressive resistance. Innovation has its inevitable hiccups, which can draw out critics. Over time, a change agent can get just plain worn down.

Everything changes in environments that celebrate creativity, welcome innovation, and accept setbacks as part of progress. Somewhat counterintuitively, it's easier for lots of teachers in a school to innovate than just one "outlier." It's easier for lots of schools in a community to innovate than just one eyebrow-raising "alternative" school. We've all heard the saying, "It takes a village to raise a child." Well, a community can come together to transform its schools.

In Newark, we met Oscar, that skinny student fighting so hard for his future. Oscar asked if I thought it was possible for adults in America to work together to make our schools great. My reaction was, "I sure hope so." Well, we're about to visit communities embracing the aspirational goal of elevating life prospects for their children, all across their region. When that happens, schools can do the impossible. These examples aren't the norm across America today, but could be. Think back to what our country's Greatest Generation pulled off. Adults in our country could join hands to help our schools and children reach their full potential. Adults could give Oscar the answer he deserves.

Cedar Rapids, Iowa—In 2012, a few members of the Cedar Rapids community asked, "What should school look like? What do we want our kids to be able to do as a result of being in school?" They created their Billy Madison project, named after a movie in which Adam Sandler goes back to school as an adult. They brought sixty-five adults, including many influential community leaders, to a high school to replicate the exact experience of a student. Not just observe for forty-five minutes. Sixty-five adults going through an entire school day treated just like students. They followed schedules with bells. They needed permission slips to use the bathroom. Desks, rows, lectures, texts, and instructions.

At the end of the day, the adults were asked, "So, what do you think?" They were appalled. Shawn Connally explained, "Our group had a CEO who spends his days making money using math. After sitting through a math class, his feedback was that the class was useless." Irrespective of income, gender, age, or politics, each participant reached the same conclusion. We can do much better. Let's define something where students choose how they use their time and what they pursue, where curriculum is integrated across disciplines, where the learning is meaningful.

With that, they launched Iowa Big.

After a summer pilot, Iowa Big started the fall semester with a dozen students, who kept one foot in their existing school while committing several hours a day to Iowa Big. This "school" has no facility or curriculum; instead, they work with over one hundred community organizations (businesses, nonprofits, policy) to identify important problems that students can help solve. Students choose which problems to attack, and the heart and soul of their school day is the work they do to improve their community.

Iowa Big draws its funding, and students, from three different Cedar Rapids (CR) school districts. The program has helped unify districts that historically viewed each other as rivals. In fact, Big is uniting the entire community, where students, teachers, and community organizations now view themselves as teams. Teachers feel more informed about the skills students will need as adults. And teachers have gained widespread respect in their community. Many now serve on the boards of partner organizations.

Troy Miller, who cofounded Iowa Big along with Connally, leads their partnership efforts. He attributes the initiative's success in part to state legislation that eliminated the Carnegie unit and lets them award credit for mastery. Assessment at Big is different, and meaningful. Partners meet frequently with students and their teacher, providing no-nonsense feedback. There's no ambiguity around the quality of student work. They need to keep working until they solve the partner's problem, or fail. Not your usual fluffy end-of-project presentation where everyone smiles, says thanks, and ignores what the students did.

"Students develop their work plan, organize it into tasks, and learn and do what's required to make progress. Individually or as teams, they work on their own for long stretches. Faculty track progress and hold them accountable for completing work, not class attendance or checking off boxes." The program doesn't work for all kids. To date, some 15% can't handle the autonomy, returning to normal school. Connally reports, though, that even these kids learn life lessons "an order of magnitude more important than turning in an essay on time."

The school has grown to 145 students with a waiting list. Of graduates to date, some 97% who applied to college were admitted to their first choice. With ties to their normal school, students have access to what's found on a normal college application (e.g., AP courses, GPA, standardized tests, extracurriculars). "But Iowa Big students also have a résumé worth looking at." One was waitlisted at the Air Force Academy and made it in against long odds. In pleading his case to the admissions officer, he emphasized his real-world experience with Big, how he struggled with team dynamics, and what he learned about leadership. These distinctive experiences "have a lot more value to many employers and colleges than a good SAT score."

Iowa Big isn't just changing the school year for its kids. Many get great summer jobs. "This year, we had a junior in high school who got a summer position at the University of Iowa hospital, beating out seventeen undergrads and thirteen postgraduates. Without his Iowa Big experience, he wouldn't have been able to get that internship. We can't take credit for his intelligence but we can take credit for giving him opportunities to be exposed to things that will take him to the next level." Miller and Connally continued, "Education is economic development if it is done well. When your students and teachers are out in the community, education is never outdated. Students are exposed to relevant problems, technologies, project management and communication methods, and resources. With education's traditional model, learning is static—not much has changed in 125 years. With this model, learning changes every day." They added, "These kids build their network and take pride in building their 'brand.' They get to know their community in new ways and appreciate it. That's really important. We have kids who used to call this place 'Cedar Crapids.' One student away for college told us, 'I'd be a fool not to come back to my network.' "

Kyle came to BIG to learn how to start a business and broaden his skill set. He started a monster.com-like website, won a competition, raised money, but the company ultimately failed. In his second year, he started working with a large local company, analyzing their distribution data using his emerging coding and database skills. "The VP asked him what he was planning to do for the summer, and he said, 'Probably wait tables.' The VP said, 'No, you're going to work for us.' He was hired as a full-time data scientist writing code to analyze their business data. When he took a computer science course at his conventional high school, he failed. Now he is getting paid a healthy salary to do something that's an 'F' on his transcript."

Isaac, an Iowa Big freshman, designed underwater submersibles, helped his school system optimize practices for students who experienced severe childhood trauma, and designed and programmed drones—in seven months. "I also had a project where I was researching genomes of different mushrooms and how to promote the commercialization of new species. A lot of my projects have been around making small apps and websites. Through that, I've been introduced to several coding languages—TSS, THP, HTML, Arduino." At age fifteen, Isaac organized a summer class for middle school kids, introducing them to different technologies—coding, Photoshop, making websites, and building drones—that he learned through Iowa Big. Pay it forward to other kids, while making three times the minimum wage. And he's already got one job offer for next summer, at a weekly salary of $760.

While Isaac's work draws on his STEM talent, Connally adds, "As a teacher, I watch Isaac doing things he thinks of as coding projects. Students often don't explicitly see how other subjects are integrated into their learning. I think about his ACES [childhood trauma] project. He's reading texts above grade level, contacting resources in the community, interviewing adults, and understanding information. This psychology project is actually three or four classes. He's well beyond a sophomore in some areas and almost done with freshman year in others. The buckets don't fill at the same rate but overall they fill faster and deeper."

Miller provided this powerful explanation for Iowa Big:

> I left a well-off school district for one that has all the classic urban problems: poverty, economics, race relations. These are issues I care deeply about. But after years of telling these students that if they can just struggle through, then they will get a job and get out of poverty. That's not true. These subjects and tests are not designed to cut the poverty cycle. As an instructor, I need to keep a pulse on what employers genuinely

want and be giving skills to students who don't have parents who can do that. Otherwise I'm just prepping them for high school courses that will prepare them for some intro college course that will prepare them for more advanced college courses that basically prepare them for nothing. Meanwhile in college, they are accumulating huge amounts of debt and will probably drop out, falling right back into the poverty trap.

Asked about pushback, Connally explained, "We actually don't get much pushback, we get volunteers. The secret is to let humans form a community and offer help when it's needed." But Big is so different that many view it cautiously. Miller adds, "To start something new has unknown outcomes. That's scary. We can come across as insane. Some pushback comes from people who believe everything has to work on a set timeline, all English classes need to read certain books. In their value system, they are right, but that's not my value system and it's not the value system of business. Other schools may believe this historical lie about assessment and grades. I don't know where that came from but someone is making a lot of money off it."

Miller concludes, "It's baffling to me that more parents don't advocate for their kids. It's fear. Fear of change, fear of what it will mean for college, and a lack of vision. I don't think it's going to come from within the school. The community needs to step up and say our students are not being prepared the way they need to be."

Ryan Wise, age thirty-nine, could easily pass for a college student. A former Mississippi TFA teacher and HGSE grad, Wise now serves as Iowa's director of education. His major initiatives are competency-based education, early literacy, teacher leadership and compensation, and Future Ready, Iowa (FRI). In discussing FRI, Wise cited a Georgetown University study that concludes that 70% of U.S. jobs by 2025 will require a higher-education degree. I questioned the premise, but Wise was unswayed. Our discussion took a curious turn later at a Des Moines community forum when I introduced Wise to Isaac from Iowa Big. Isaac described the skills he's already acquired as a high school freshman, to Wise's amazement. At age fifteen, Isaac is more prepared than most recent college graduates for getting a great job, being a thoughtful citizen, and making his world better. He may end up going to college, but his Iowa Big education makes that optional.

Your school might not be up for something as ambitious as Cedar Rapids' Billy Madison project, but you can start small with help from School Retool, an outstanding nonprofit created by Stanford's d.school, the Hewlett Foundation (funder of the Deeper Learning initiative), and IDEO (leaders in design thinking). School Retool's mission is to help schools create cultures of innovation. Their Shadow a Student campaign has sparked thousands of adults, usually principals, to walk in a student's shoes for an entire day and then share reflections with their community. Drawing on their resources, you could invite community leaders to your school to shadow a student or a teacher. Like the civic leaders in Cedar Rapids, they could become your staunchest allies.

Atlanta, Georgia—After a thirteen-year business career, Laura Deisley moved into education, concerned that schools aren't preparing kids for the world they'll live in. After leading strategic innovation for a top private school, in 2012 she cofounded the Atlanta K–12 Design Challenge, bringing design thinking and innovation skills to public and private schools. Building on these successes, she set out to create "a model that would have the disciplines more integrated and the student learning experience more project-based, choice-based, and connected to experts and the world outside the classroom."

Deisley's Lab Atlanta is a semester school located in downtown Atlanta. It draws high school sophomores from all over this large metropolitan area, giving them the opportunity to "imagine Atlanta as your classroom—a classroom without walls." Students invent projects to help create a sustainable future for their city—addressing air and water quality, public transportation, shared resources, and poverty. Their interdisciplinary curriculum challenges students to research, think, argue, and defend. They bring local youth together, "helping them learn to look at the city and their world with empathy (and less 'other'), and empowering them with design and innovation skills—a way to build bridges and foster hope. It's about believing we can—at any age—be change agents for good."

Students committing to Lab Atlanta aren't making a big bet. It's a semester, not all of high school. Sophomore year is the most interruptible of the high school years. Students with athletic proficiency have the flexibility to pick the semester when they aren't playing their favorite sport. With ambitious scholarship offerings, their student body reflects Atlanta's full diversity—a melting pot of kids who live together, collaborate, and become lifelong friends.

At scale, Lab Atlanta will have one hundred students each semester. While that may sound modest, it's a brilliant Trojan horse. At each semester's Exhibition Night, students present their work to friends, family, teachers, administrators, and influential community members from all over the city. As a broad cross-section of Atlanta sees the impact of PEAK learning, Lab Atlanta is reshaping education priorities across an entire six-million-person city.

Oklahoma City, Oklahoma—"Creative Oklahoma" seems like a contender for Oxymoron of the Year. If you haven't been there, you might preface "Oklahoma" with adjectives like flat, dusty, hot, maybe even boring. But creative it is, and fun to visit.

Sir Ken Robinson is a force working behind the scenes for Oklahoma. Robinson grew up in working-class England. Challenged at age four with polio, he went on to become the world's voice on the importance of creativity. Sir Ken electrified the annual TED conference in 2006 with his "Do Schools Kill Creativity?" talk. Full of humorous anecdotes, he delivers a body blow to standardized education:

> The result is that we are educating people out of their creative capacities. Picasso once said this, he said that all children are born artists. The problem is to remain an artist as we grow up. I believe this passionately, that we don't grow into creativity, we grow out of it. Or rather, we get educated out of it.

Sir Ken's inspiring message has been a singular force for change in our schools. His talk has been viewed forty million times online, and is every bit as relevant today as it was in 2006. I'm always surprised when someone involved in education hasn't seen it. Yet I met with a senior U.S. Senate staff member with education power who had never heard of Sir Ken. A bit like being on the Rock and Roll Hall of Fame induction committee and not knowing of the Beatles.

Creative Oklahoma, with its website www.stateofcreativity.com, sponsors annual awards to educators, artists, entrepreneurs, students, and organizations for creating powerful learning environments. Their Oklahoma Innovation Series brings international leaders to the state to share insights about creativity. They convene networking gatherings—big and small—across the state. They support research and professional training on how to foster creativity. Bold and brash, they're reshaping Oklahoma's landscape. Creative Oklahoma is on to an issue facing all organizations today: a dearth of creative employees. In one forum, a top executive of a leading defense contractor told me, "Our HR department won't interview anyone unless they have a college degree with a minimum GPA of 3.75. Our biggest concern is a lack of creativity in our workforce. This discussion makes me think that we might be weeding out some of our most innovative applicants."

Oklahoma derives value from unlikely sources. With no hills to its name, it's home to the whitewater training center for the U.S. Olympic team. Ravaged by vicious tornadoes, Oklahoma is the location of the National Weather Museum. Its interminable 375-mile stretch of Route 66 is punctuated by funky roadside museums, drive-ins, and old-style filling stations. The site of the 1995 bombing of the Alfred P. Murrah Federal Building—with 168 deaths, 680 serious injuries, and damage to 324 buildings in a sixteen-block radius—is home to the stunning Oklahoma City National Memorial Museum honoring victims, survivors, and rescuers. The museum's education offerings are extraordinary, with compelling physical displays and interactive simulations. Visitors walk in the shoes of a forensic expert, gain hands-on experience in powdering and analyzing fingerprints, cast dental stone, and extract DNA using household items. Drawn in, kids learn how chemistry and biology helped convict the perpetrators of the largest act of terrorism committed in our country by U.S. citizens. The museum is telling "a story that needs to be told so that there's a better tomorrow."

Creative Oklahoma is "helping schools think, plan, and behave more creatively." They're bringing experiential learning to schools across the state, and working to ensure that the arts are prominent. They support research, offer programs to foster collaboration, and award prizes for student creativity. They're helping schools implement next-generation assessments that recognize competency and creativity in student work. Creative Oklahoma is making headway creatively, not with a few schools and students but all across the state.

When I started this trip, I expected to see the best examples of education innovation in progressive states with lots of high-tech—Massachusetts, California, and New York. I anticipated that conservative states would be, well, conservative when it comes to school. But I found remarkable innovation in places like North Dakota, Kentucky, and Oklahoma. Locations flooded with tech start-ups were, on balance, reluctant to rethink school, perhaps victims of a history of success with the old model.

_ _ _ _ _   \\|/   _ _ _ _ _

Pittsburgh, Pennsylvania—Pittsburgh evokes a certain feeling of community. Their citywide transformation from a grimy steel town into an architectural gem, the undying loyalty they hold for their sports teams, and their abundance of local philanthropy. So it shouldn't be surprising that across all of America, Pittsburgh is leading the way in bringing together their community to reimagine learning for their children.

Pittsburgh's foundations focus on local issues and stay close to their roots. Education leadership there comes from the Grable Foundation, founded by the widow of a 1930s venture capitalist from Pittsburgh, who invested in a little start-up called Rubber-Maid. Grable's CEO is modest and soft-spoken Gregg Behr, who joined the foundation in 2006. He brings competence and leadership to his role and looks so huggable that he should be thankful that his parents didn't give him my first name. Upon joining Grable, Behr conducted a listening tour across "Steeler Nation," meeting with teachers, librarians, and youth advocates to understand how his foundation could best serve Pittsburgh.

Behr kept hearing about rapid changes in the way kids are learning. "Adults would tell me that they weren't connecting with kids the same way they did as recently as a year or two ago." He met with learning scientists and found that cognitive science shows that today's kids are "remarkably different. The way they develop their identities and goals, the way they consume and produce information, are happening differently. It's driven by available technology. It gave me pause because if, in fact, kids are fundamentally different, it means we have to think about learning drastically differently."

In 2007, Behr brought a dozen people together for a pancake breakfast at Pamela's to exchange views on the future of learning. This "electric conversation" led to forming a "Kids + Creativity" group, which snowballed. They borrowed a gong from the Pittsburgh Symphony and hosted an event where "people got three minutes to deliver lightning talks, and we'd gong them off the stage if they went over." These meetings evolved into Pittsburgh's Remake Learning Network, now encompassing 250 schools, museums, libraries, and learning centers, and 3,000 active professionals from a wide range of disciplines. Behr notes, "We didn't set out to create a network. We just wanted to do right for our kids."

In forming this coalition, they consciously embraced "the messiness of language. We didn't get caught up in definitions of what Remake Learning was. If STEM or STEAM or Maker or tech-enhanced learning or whatever pedagogical approach made sense for you, it made sense for us, provided it encourages modern learning at the core—hands-on learning that develops critical thinking, deconstructing problem solving, iterative design, and learning together. Remake Learning became an umbrella."

Remake Learning strives to give all Pittsburgh kids access to resources like makerspaces, robotics programs, toy design, and multimedia tools to create works of art. They want to make learning authentic and genuine for children who are surrounded by caring adults who understand that "if a kid is lit up by an experience, build on it." They offer professional training resources to teachers, empowering them to be Remake Learning leaders. They're establishing a system of credentials and badges to capture emerging skills. They use their city as a platform to enhance learning experiences, connecting classrooms with more than 200 participating organizations providing remarkable support, like BirdBrain Technologies donating 1,000 robots to Pittsburgh libraries.

A few years ago, Remake Learning hosted an event for Pittsburgh school superintendents to meet Don Marinelli, the cofounder of the Entertainment Tech Center (ETC) at Carnegie Mellon. Bart Rocco showed up. He heads the low-income Elizabeth Ford School District in what used to be a thriving industrial center in the Monongahela Valley. Inspired, Rocco secured a microgrant from Grable to create classroom space mirroring the ETC. Behr reported, "Within a year, over 25% of their students enrolled. It was immediate affirmation that something was happening." They subsequently invested in "learning by doing" makerspaces and tech labs. Participation in summer learning programs increased 500%, enrollment in nearby charter schools dropped by two-thirds, and they went from dozens of dropouts to none. Even though they don't teach to the test, student scores increased. "They've created an environment where kids want to be in school." Their progress has been contagious. Sixty-seven other Pittsburgh school districts have since secured similar microgrants to catalyze innovation.

School is just one of the places where students learn, and Remake Learning set out to prepare parents and caregivers for helping outside of school hours. To reach them, Behr knew that they "needed media partnerships with magazines and radio stations. We needed to do something much more personal in our outreach to families." These insights led to Remake Learning Week. I was invited to Pittsburgh to screen *MLTS* at the Carnegie Science Center as the week was kicking off. In walking around a beautiful downtown with its classic architecture, I found "Remake Learning" banners everywhere—rallying energy for a week that's part festival, part professional development, and part uplifting community celebration of authentic learning. Behr's "hope was that there would be one hundred events. There ended up being nearly three hundred events during the week, with nearly thirty thousand people attending. We hired community organizers to ensure there were events and marketing in our low-income and rural neighborhoods. Six of the seven zip codes where we saw the highest levels of participation were low-income zip codes. We ended up securing 140 different commitments from 97 different organizations totaling at least $25 million in support for the coming year to support the Remake Learning Network."

Over the past decade, Grable has invested roughly $25 million in Remake Learning. Behr likes "working regionally. I like knowing personally these communities and people. We are only getting to the place we're at because of ten years of being patient and doing the work of relationship building. I tell folks I don't know if it will take other cities ten years, but it takes patience to invest in a community in this way." Grable's impressive work now draws visitors from across America to learn more about how engaged citizens can collaborate to elevate learning across their community.

Behr closed by telling me, "I have two daughters, five and two. I will have failed my own kids horribly if they have a school experience just like mine."

Honolulu, Hawai'i—Prior to setting out on this trip, my wife and I talked about its challenges for our family. She's incredibly supportive of what I'm doing and had just a few requests. I'd be home for holidays with our children. I'd return if health issues arose for either of our elderly mothers. And she asked if we could finish in Hawai'i and add an extra week for vacation. So I arrived in Honolulu with a preconceived notion of what would constitute success. After having seen so much, I didn't expect anything to stand out. My game plan was simple. Power through, finish the trip, and relax. That would define success in Hawai'i.

But Hawai'i didn't work out that way.

Months in advance, my team used superlatives in describing citizen volunteer Josh Reppun and his support for *MLTS* in Hawai'i. Reppun is a former teacher turned top sales consultant in Oahu's flagship Apple Store, with a twenty-five-year-old daughter off and running in life on the mainland. With no immediate family ties to Hawai'i schools, he spends every spare minute fighting to advance learning in his native state. In planning my weeklong visit, he organized an exceptional itinerary with several out-of-the-box endeavors—an eleven-person podcast on the future of education, a morning session with students and human resources officers to design a modern résumé, and a parent workshop based on clips from *MLTS*. He even managed to produce the documentary *Ka Helena A'o: The Learning Walk* about my visit.

Reppun was determined to set up a meeting with Governor David Ige and the First Lady, which I assumed would fall into the category of "best-laid plans." But four days before flying to Honolulu, he indicated he'd arranged for a brief meeting during the only schedule slot that worked on all fronts—Sunday morning on Mother's Day. When we showed up at the governor's mansion, I expected a quick "Hi. Here's a lei. Aloha." An hour and a half later, it began to dawn on me that something special was happening in Hawai'i.

With backgrounds in technology, innovation, and teaching, Hawai'i's governor and First Lady bring an informed perspective to education. The First Lady taught elementary school for years and offered profound insights into classroom practices, student potential, and the impact of testing and accountability policies. While many describe David Ige as reserved, he was animated in describing the importance of education to his state and the need for innovation. He was particularly energized about the impact of a teacher he's supported for two decades, Candy Suiso.

In 1997, with discarded camera equipment and an empty broom closet, Suiso founded a media program at Wai'anae High School, located in one of Oahu's poorest communities. Now housed in two buildings with major new construction underway, she and her 250 students are immersed in journalism, video production, website design, graphic design, digital marketing, and entrepreneurial ventures. The energy level of her students is off the charts, with a long history of distinguished awards. At the national Student Television Network competition, some forty Wai'anae students blew away attendees. One outsider asked, "Are these kids from your state's top private high school?" The stereotypes people hold. Suiso's transformational program has launched careers and businesses across the islands, helping her state become a global leader in media arts.

With Reppun's help, I visited one spectacular school after another, all across Hawai'i. They were all types (public, private, and charter), with kids of all backgrounds, achieving impressive results in all sorts of ways. One features experiential learning on a voyaging canoe in Hawai'i's Pacific waters. Another on Hawai'i Island's Kona Coast has a nature theme including an on-campus shark tank, one-upping schools with programs based on the show *Shark Tank*. At one school, a team of aspiring young journalists interviewed me to produce a news report for PBS Hawai'i, with support from PBS's remarkable *HIKI NŌ* program. A school on the Big Island features a spectacular science center showcasing world-class student research. A middle school is organized around students tackling essential questions. These visits were like watching the finale of the Fourth of July fireworks celebration—one spectacular burst of innovation after another.

At Waipahu High School (WHS), led by Keith Hayashi, a student told me how proud they were to be from the community "we know the rest of our state describes as the ghetto of Hawai'i. We know our families are poor. But we also know we're going to do great things in life, and we'll do it with support from our families and classmates." The school combines academics with career paths—arts and communication, business services, health services, industrial engineering technology, natural resources, and public and human services. As an example of achievement, a Waipahu team won the "Best in State" Verizon App Challenge award for "My Choice," a mobile app that lets students, faculty, and staff communicate issues to the administration in a timely and private way.

Hayashi walked me through his school's four-year sequence. During the first two years, students focus on an academic base and are organized into "houses" connected to a support team of faculty and peers. Upperclassmen can plug into a career pathway connected to local business partners and real-world problems. Some four hundred are taking college classes—at either Leeward Community College or the University of Hawai'i at West Oahu—with tuition covered by the generous McInerny Foundation.

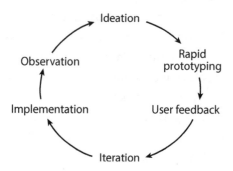

FIGURE 10.1. IDEO's Human-Centered Design Process. *Source*: "IDEO'S 6-Step Human-Centered Design Process: How to Make Things People Want" by Spencer Lanoue, www.usertesting.com. July 9, 2015.

Several WHS students have become experts in Human-Centered Design, with help from local tech guru Ian Kitajima of Oceanit. The design thinking process was pioneered by IDEO, the Silicon Valley consulting firm whose body of work includes inventing the original computer mouse for Steve Jobs. These Waipahu students delivered an impressive explanation of their methodology, then jumped into action, leading a process to create ways to pay tribute to alumni who lost their lives in the Vietnam War. In an hour, they had generated a wide suite of ideas, artfully weeded out clunkers, synthesized the best themes, and zeroed in on creating a mural at a local rail station alongside a memorial park with a tree and a bench for each fallen soldier. Each bench would include a plaque with a QR code, linking to photos and a written history of fallen alumni.

I encouraged these students to use their design-thinking expertise to create summer jobs. Pitch Hawaiian Electric on leading a design-thinking process about how best to engage teenagers to help manage residential energy usage. Lead a project for the local bank on establishing lifelong relationships with teenagers. I told them, "Prepare a presentation like the one I just saw, use your network to get to the CEO, pitch them, and close the deal by saying, 'We normally charge $25,000 for a project of this scope, but because you're a great corporate citizen, we'll do this for $10,000.' "

These Waipahu kids are deeply grateful to their families, teachers, and school. I noticed kids on this nondescript campus stopping to pick up trash to keep the grounds immaculate—something unusual at high schools. They're on a crusade to do something with their lives, to make their community proud, to live up to their school's motto: "My Voice. My Choice. My Future."

In a walk across the campus of Honolulu's Mid-Pacific Institute, I fell in with upper-school principal Tom McManus. He related that his faculty has been wrestling with the question "What does quality look like in your discipline?" This wasn't a casual lunch discussion. Last year, faculty explored this topic for six separate three-hour meetings, growing convinced that this "conversation about quality will remain on the agenda forever. It's recursive and ongoing. It's key to empowering teachers as professionals." In tackling this question, Mid-Pacific puts teachers in the leadership role in defining standards for assessing quality in their discipline. For example,

> The Language Arts teachers pulled writing samples from all K–12 classrooms and collectively sorted them into "Low-Medium-High." The teachers then identified evidence in each paper for why it belonged in a certain place. Each grade level identified a set of anchor papers showing a continuum of progress. These anchor papers serve as a guide to students

who can self-assess their own quality against the samples. Because the continuum goes all the way through, there is always a next step for the student to measure herself against and attempt to improve.

I shared with him the similarity between their approach and how the state of New Hampshire is implementing next-generation assessments. McManus stressed the importance of students participating "in their own assessment. They need to have an idea of what quality work looks like, have time to practice and work toward it, and take ownership of their next learning steps. We believe that grading and measuring every step of that process is demotivating and counter to lifelong learning."

Mid-Pacific's exploration led naturally to the topic of grades. McManus notes, "Assessment drives education and it's much more complicated than most educators want to admit." As teachers laid out their assessment framework, they realized that grades reflect factors unrelated to work quality—factors like effort, positive attitude, persistence, attendance, class participation, and meeting deadlines. Or things he didn't mention—like working the system and playing up to the teacher. While some are important life skills, McManus argues that they shouldn't drive the grade in a discipline. To frame this, imagine a student who produces exceptional work in all subjects but always hands in assignments late. Should her report card be full of Bs and Cs, or should she get an A in each discipline and an F in time management?

This discussion of quality crystallized much of what I observed this year. Let's classify student work into two categories: Direct Quality and Indirect Quality.

> *Direct Quality*: Students produce work whose quality can be directly assessed—art courses (photography, film, dance, theater), CTE courses (welding, computer programming, woodworking), after-school activities (school newspaper, yearbook, athletic perfor-

mance), and some mainstream humanities courses (thought-ful essays, creative writing).

Indirect Quality: Students sequence through content, concepts, formulas, and procedures—and are tested on recall, pattern recognition, and the ability to replicate low-level procedures. Their work *indirectly* reflects aspects of learning, but they don't produce original work. There's an underlying assump-tion that Indirect Quality assignments enable a student, at some future point, to produce Direct Quality work—but this assumption is seldom, if ever, validated.

I often ask people, "When you think back on your school years, what experiences made you the person you are today?" Without ex-ception, adults point to Direct Quality endeavors. Yet our grade 7–12 students spend almost all of their time on Indirect Quality tasks. PEAK vs. anti-PEAK—education's tale of two cities.

My final official event in Hawai'i was an *MLTS* screening to some of the state's most influential leaders. This would be the last of more than seventy-five screenings I did during this travel year, so my adrenaline was pumping. I introduced the film, watched for a few minutes to check the sound level, and headed off for a long walk. I was in the parking lot when an older gentleman came out early, never a good sign. He saw me and walked over to introduce himself. The CEO of Hawaiian Electric explained, "I've seen the film before and love it. It was important to me to be here tonight to show support, but my daughter just went into labor. I hope you'll under-stand if I leave early to be there for the birth of my grandchild."

I wish the evening had had a rousing finale. Maybe it did. When *MLTS* plays, I'm always in the room to watch the last five minutes. I won't give away the ending, but I never grow tired of it. That night, as the film entered its final blow-you-away stretch, I said to the stranger next to me, "Fasten your seatbelt. This film goes into hy-perdrive right about . . . now." And I timed "now" to coincide with the narrator saying "irrefutable fact." At that exact moment, the DVD froze. Yikes! After so many glitch-free screenings, a hiccup on my very last tour event. No way. I figure we'll clean off the DVD, skip a few seconds ahead, and sort this out quickly. But after ten minutes of tech-savvy effort, it's clear we were out of luck. With no choice but to make the best of it, I go up front and walk them through the film's last few minutes, which I repeat verbatim. We then have an outstanding discussion with people who, collectively, can transform Hawai'i's schools.

As we were about to call it a night, one merciful person offered this final comment. "We're so happy the DVD stopped. We have unfinished work to do here in Hawai'i to make our schools great and hope you'll come back." One of those creative acts of kindness I've come to expect in this great state, from this great trip.

I promised my wife that I'd steer clear of education during our vacation week. The topic came up, though, when we were on a small catamaran with a dozen strangers exploring Kaua'i's north side. A woman explained to the group that she had spent her career teaching but retired two years earlier. I was tempted to jump in, but my wife's sharp elbow persuaded me to keep silent. So I just listened as she ended with, "You know, teaching used to be a craft. Now it's all about standardized tests. So I retired early." In the worst way, I wanted to tell her about schools across Hawai'i, across the country. About what school could be.

OK, maybe my trip, and this book, should finish in Hawai'i, where so many inspiring things happened. But after nine months of travel, I had great stories to share from forty-nine states across America. One state, though, was my nemesis. I decided to return.

_ _ _ _ _   \\|/⁄   _ _ _ _ _

Rapid City, Rosebud, and Pierre, South Dakota—I had my challenges in South Dakota. I spent two days here early in the trip but did a lousy job of planning the visit. I ended up cold-calling several schools and educators but struck out in finding anything innovative. In the film *MLTS*, a student keeps coming back to finish a project. I thought it'd be cool to mirror that. Return to South Dakota after my trip was "officially" finished and pull off a surprise end.

Getting to this state, by the way, is no picnic. In mid-June, bone tired, I flew back to Rapid City and then drove through a downpour to Murdo. After a few hours of sleep, I left early the next morning for the Rosebud Indian reservation to address their Tribal Indian Council about possibilities for their schools. First up, though, the Council heard from Larry, who runs Ed & Larry's Auto Repair. Larry advocated for having students serve as apprentices with local businesses, something that might strike you as minor. But I took it as one more encouraging reflection of grassroots insight into how best to educate our kids.

That afternoon I drove to Pierre, home to South Dakota's beautiful State Capitol for a meeting with Melody Schopp, their secretary of education. Given how things had gone for me in here, I braced for some last-minute glitch. But Schopp was terrific. Articulate and energetic, she epitomized what I saw in every state across the country: talented, dedicated, and visionary people fighting for the best possible futures for their kids.

And with that, the trip was both officially and unofficially over, ending appropriately. My time here reminds us of the work ahead. There are amazing classrooms all across America, but they're still not easy to find. Yet.

Reflections

I took this trip because I had things to say to America, and things I hoped to learn. I wanted to sound alarm bells about a tsunami of innovation heading our way, with profound ramifications for our children and schools. And I hoped to learn from teachers about what makes for a great classroom and how to create them at scale. While it's easy to fault my execution, I did make it to all fifty states. I met one-on-one with a dozen governors, half the education committee heads for state legislatures, and half the commissioners of education. I met over one hundred thousand students, teachers, parents, and just plain citizens.

Looking back, the trip was different, better, and more inspiring than I ever imagined. Like so much we do in life, clarity came after the fact. At the start, I was pessimistic about our country's prospects for transforming education. Systems are hard to change. The model is entrenched. Our metrics are familiar and accepted. Our national education leaders want to manage the system, not reimagine it. But as the months rolled by, optimism crept in. For starters, no one—and I mean no one—defends the status quo. People realize that our schools need to change. Every community has teachers, parents, citizen volunteers, and philanthropists working tirelessly on behalf of their children. Today, most think it's a matter of execution—do the same old things better. But a growing number recognize that we need to do better things. They can be an unstoppable force.

If you're looking for eye-popping optimism, spend time with young children. They're natural learners, brimming with curiosity, audacity, and creativity. Again and again, adults would share, "You know, nowadays, a child that gets interested in something can become an expert in a matter of days." This simple, staggering observation is knocking on the front door of every school in America. Time to let it in.

In fields like cancer research and nuclear fusion, experts have yet to find breakthroughs. In education, our experts know what to do. The problem is, we listen to the wrong experts. Our innovative teachers, not those at the top of the education pyramid, are the ones who know. They're creating classrooms where children thrive, where students are building purpose, essential skills, agency, and authentic knowledge. They're willing to stand up to those eight damaging words: "We have to be able to measure it." They understand that ranking our children requires standardizing their education. And when you standardize education, you rob students of any opportunity to go deep on what they care about, to build distinctive competencies, and to create differentiated paths

TABLE 11.1 U.S. Education: The Old and (Perhaps) the New

Century-Old Model	A New Vision
Industrial	Innovative
Centralized	Decentralized
Data-driven	Purpose-driven
Micromanaged Classrooms	Trusted Classrooms
Standardized Curriculum	Organic Learning
Drill	Create
Content and Low-Level Skills	Essential Skill Sets and Mind-sets
College Ready	Life Ready

forward—the very things that will enable them to thrive in the innovation era. The very essence of the American Dream.

My trip coincided with the 2016 presidential election. In some twenty-four primary and presidential debates, education got about fourteen seconds of attention. Nevertheless, the election was all about U.S. education. On any side of any aisle, millions are angry, alienated, and adrift. They're financially vulnerable, unable to piece together any semblance of a career. Irrespective of education level, they struggle to parse a blizzard of misbegotten claims and sketchy newsfeeds. Thoughtful debate and collaboration have all but disappeared from the national stage. Voters fear that they and their children are destined for the wrong end of life's bell curve.

But don't think for a minute that Americans have given up on the future. They care, desperately. All across our country, I saw people's passion for their children and their schools. They'd do cartwheels if a candidate offered a compelling message about education, the very foundation of our democracy. They long for a speech like this:

My fellow Americans. Our country has never been more divided—in outlook, in financial means, in life prospects. While our GDP is growing, gains are concentrated among our wealthiest. For the rest, median wages are flat, millions live paycheck-to-paycheck, and record numbers have given up looking for work. America in the twenty-first century: "The best of times for a few. The worst of times for the many."

With Americans suffering, it's easy to blame immigrants, or trade deals, or terrorists. These ignorant words fire people up but lead us astray. We need to understand how our world is being shaped by innovation, automation, and machine intelligence. Low-skilled jobs aren't going to Mexico or China or immigrants—they're just plain going away. While our roads and trains need repair, it's our crumbling education infrastructure that jeopardizes our futures. We need schools to prepare Americans—rich and poor, young and old—for the future, not the past.

Founded as the land of equal opportunity, our nation leads the developed world in childhood poverty. In America today, a child's prospects depend more on birth circumstance than character. Education further tilts the imbalance. We can change this. Our babies and toddlers need high-quality early care and education. Our K–12 schools, particularly in our low-income neighborhoods, need the resources to educate their students. We can make the high school diploma stand for something important—graduates equipped with real career and citizenship skills. Our education system can regain its historic role in helping level America's playing field.

Our teachers can lead the way in transforming our schools, but they can't do it alone. Education is a community's responsibility. I'm asking adults to volunteer time and expertise to help our children, especially those in challenging circumstances. Support preschool programs. Connect students to internships, summer jobs, mentors, and real-world problems. Trust and respect our teachers. Listen and learn from them.

We need to rethink the role of college. Each year, online resources make it easier and easier to learn on your own, yet we push kids to spend more and more years in costly formal education. This doesn't make sense. I respect the contributions of our Ivory Tower academicians, but they've taken over U.S. education. Colleges charge exorbitant tuition levels and cater to the affluent. We've turned K–12 education into thirteen years of preparing kids for college, not life. This needs to end.

Our country's fifteen hundred community colleges can accelerate career prospects for adults, young and old. Unlike academic four-year colleges, they're grounded in practice. I'm calling on them to offer short-term immersive learning experiences that equip students with decisive career skills. We need tax incentives for U.S. businesses to modernize their workforce. Everyone wins if employees in dead-end jobs have the opportunity to acquire advanced skills rather than punch the clock until they're laid off.

The innovation era plays to America's strengths. We're the most creative, inventive society on the planet. We lead the world in Nobel prizes, in music, in art, in patents, in technology, in innovative start-ups, in social entrepreneurship. Our country is in the perfect position to thrive. But getting on the right side of innovation has to start with education. In 1893, America had the courage to transform schools to prepare young adults for a world of manufacturing. Let us once again have the courage to transform our schools, to launch our children into lives of purpose, to unleash their potential to create a better future for all.

Don't hold your breath. We're not likely to hear this from a politician soon, maybe ever. State and national policies may never make much sense. We'll only be exasperated if we expect real change to come from our putative leaders. But here's the deal. Schools won't change from the top. They'll change one classroom, one school, one district at a time. And local change is achievable change.

Who knows if America will rise to this challenge? I don't, even after this immersive trip. We may hold to the myth that real learning happens in our schools, that test scores tell us what we need to know, and that a college degree bestows magical capabilities to the fortunate few who can access and afford it. We may convince ourselves that the ravages of machine intelligence are a century away, so there's no urgency for reimagining school. If these views prevail, our civil society is headed for collapse.

But America just may step up. I love the phrase "Change happens slowly, right up until it happens quickly." I saw signs this year that America is at an inflection point. People are connecting the dots. They're starting to see that we need to do better things in our schools, for our children. They're sensing the unbounded possibilities if we turn our students loose on problems they care about. They're ready to trust our teachers to engage and inspire our students. And as I learned so emphatically on this trip, once someone sees what school could be, there's no turning back. Oscar, don't give up on us.

Acknowledgments

Many people made this book possible. It builds on the brilliant work of Greg Whiteley, Adam Leibowitz, Adam Ridley, and Gabe Patay, who created the film *Most Likely to Succeed*. Tony Wagner, my coauthor on the book *Most Likely to Succeed: Preparing Our Kids for the Innovation Era*, has been a major voice for reimagining education. I can't imagine this journey without his expertise and inspiration.

It took a team to orchestrate a trip with such complicated logistics. Special and huge thanks to Jeff Johnson of Riverwood Strategies, and to Andrea Houlne and Andrea Iacolucci. They made this possible. Added logistical help came from The Future Project's Nora Parent and Andrew Mangino. Susan Oliver worked tirelessly to connect me with local media every step of the way.

I am deeply grateful to the dedicated, amazing citizen volunteers who helped plan my visits across the country. I wish space allowed me to tell readers more about them and their many contributions. From the bottom of my heart, I thank Brad Wilson in Michigan, Eric Wilson in Arkansas, Sherri Oberg in New Hampshire, Brad Oliver in Indiana, John Moore in Delaware, Jonathan Kreiss-Tomkins and Bob Miller in Alaska, Barbara Bellissimo and Carmen Coleman in Kentucky, Greg Tehven in North Dakota, Kristie Jochmann in Wisconsin, Kanya Balakrishna in New Jersey, Sam Seidel in Rhode Island, Andrew Frishman in several states, Jon Bacal in Minnesota, Barbara Caldwell in North Carolina, Kami

Dmitrova in Connecticut, Bob and Christi Worsley in Arizona, Temp Keller in Texas, Andrew Brennen in Kentucky and West Virginia, and the indefatigable Josh Reppun in Hawai'i. Each of you went to the ends of the earth to organize my time in your state, set up great meetings, and inspire me to do more.

Thanks to the many people who helped in bringing this manuscript to its finish line. Of the many who offered comments on my progressive set of drafts, special thanks to Tamara Day, Andy Payne, Lynda Weinman, Andrew Mangino, Jacqui Lipson, Esmond Harmsworth, Laura McBain, Sam Seidel, Esther Hong Delaney, Helen Morey, and Suzanne McGee. Janet Goldstein helped me navigate the complicated world of book publishing. To Vickie Kearn, my champion at Princeton University Press, I am deeply grateful for your support, advice, and enthusiasm for this work. Her colleagues Ellen Foos and Jenn Backer were also exceptionally helpful in bringing this book into being.

Finally, huge thanks to my family. My mom and my mother-in-law brought enthusiasm and good cheer to my work. Sadly, they both passed away shortly after this trip's conclusion. My wife, Elizabeth Hazard, is supportive and loving beyond words. She traveled with me for part of the trip and helps me every day, in so many ways. She offered many suggestions along the way, and her outgoing nature prompted her to strike up a conversation with a perfect stranger in a restaurant, who happened to work for an outstanding publisher, who happened to be Vickie Kearn. My two children also support my work and make me proud of them every single day as they forge unconventional paths forward.

And with that, I bring this book to its close.

Notes

1. http://www.politifact.com/punditfact/statements/2015/jun/09/hunter
-schwarz/47-say-they-lack-ready-cash-pay-surprise-400-bill/.
2. https://www2.ed.gov/pubs/NatAtRisk/risk.html.
3. http://www.nytimes.com/1992/02/06/us/american-children-trail-in-math
-and-science.html.
4. Janelle Duray, private communication with the author, Jobs for Americas Graduates, August 12, 2017.
5. http://www.press.uchicago.edu/ucp/books/book/chicago/A/bo10327226.html
or in the e-book at location 814 of 5486. Also from the book *Academically Adrift*, ebook, location 814 of 5486: "From their freshman entrance to the end of their sophomore year, students in our sample on average have improved these skills, as measured by the CLA [College Learning Assessment], by only 0.18 standard deviation. This translates into a seven percentile point gain."
6. http://www.acha-ncha.org/docs/NCHA-II_WEB_SPRING_2015_REFER ENCE_GROUP_EXECUTIVE_SUMMARY.pdf.
7. https://economix.blogs.nytimes.com/2010/07/16/yale-harvard-law-taking
-over-supreme-court/?_r=0.
8. https://mic.com/articles/132995/new-report-shows-just-how-unequal-the
-college-admissions-process-actually-is#.OWO3f7RrX.
9. https://www.nytimes.com/interactive/2017/01/18/upshot/some-colleges
-have-more-students-from-the-top-1-percent-than-the-bottom-60.html.
10. https://blogs.wsj.com/economics/2014/10/07/sat-scores-and-income
-inequality-how-wealthier-kids-rank-higher/.
11. https://www.theatlantic.com/business/archive/2013/04/heres-how-little
-math-americans-actually-use-at-work/275260/.
12. http://changetheequation.org/press/new-survey-americans-say-%E2%80
%9Cwe%E2%80%99re-not-good-math%E2%80%9D.
13. https://www.forbes.com/sites/nickmorgan/2012/10/30/the-best-speech
-about-education-ever/#5118efef1fa4.
14. https://books.google.com/books?id=2XH-BlKg_UwC&pg=PT98&lpg=PT
98&dq=We+live+today,+crowded+together,+in+a+culture+overloaded
+with+information,+surfeited+with+data+and+opinions+and+experiences
+that+we+pump+up+with+the+buttons+on+our+TV+sets,+home+com
puters,+telephones,+and+word+processors.&source=bl&ots=PicD4-V8
Zv&sig=KMfSLGW2koOh1ankdk3IQl_NKcY&hl=en&sa=X&ved=0ahUKE
wio0MzXztnVAhVI4WMKHeT3C2IQ6AEIKDAA#v=onepage.
15. https://www.nmefoundation.org/global/featured-research/research-land
ing-page/policy-barriers-to-school-improvement-what-s-real.

Index

NOTE: Page numbers followed by *f* indicate a figure. Those followed by *t* indicate a table.

About the Author

Ted Dintersmith is a change agent focused on the impact of education and innovation on the future of civil society. His professional background spans technology, entrepreneurship, and public policy. He was ranked by Business 2.0 as the top-performing U.S. venture capitalist for 1995-1999. In 2012, President Obama appointed him to represent our country at the United Nations General Assembly. More recently, he executive produced the acclaimed documentary Most Likely to Succeed and co-authored with Tony Wagner a book with the same title. In 2018, he received NEA's prestigious "Friend of Education" Award. Ted earned a PhD in Engineering from Stanford and an undergraduate degree from the College of William and Mary, with High Honors in Physics and English. When he's not visiting schools, he lives in central Virginia.

Innovation Playlist
small steps lead to big change

The Innovation Playlist is a resource that helps your school reimagine its future, and supports your informed innovations to move forward. Just as Spotify's libraries of songs, albums, and playlists let you craft and share great listening experiences, the Innovation Playlist offers:

- Small pedagogical steps (think songs) that draw on the proven work of remarkable teachers and organizations. Each has a short video bringing you up to speed, and requires modest amounts of class time (as short as 20 minutes) -- minimal downside and boundless upside.

- Sequences (think albums) of small steps that lead to a big change on an important priority.

Start your journey now at
www.InnovationPlaylist.org